INFORMATION AND MIND

CSLI Lecture Notes Number 229

INFORMATION AND MIND

THE PHILOSOPHY OF FRED DRETSKE

edited by
PAUL SKOKOWSKI

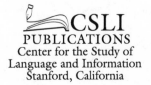
CSLI
PUBLICATIONS
Center for the Study of
Language and Information
Stanford, California

Library of Congress Cataloging-in-Publication Data

Names: Skokowski, Paul, editor.

Title: Information and mind : the philosophy of Fred Dretske / [edited] by Paul
   Skokowski.

Description: Stanford, California : CSLI Publications, [2020] | Series: CSLI Lecture
   Notes, 229 | Includes bibliographical references and index. | Summary:"The
   papers in this volume examine several topics that Fred Dretske addressed in his
   philosophical career. These papers range from one of the earliest problems Fred
   addressed, the nature of seeing an object, to epistemological issues that Fred
   worked on from mid-career onwards, to issues he focused on later in his career,
   including information, mental representation, and conscious experience"–
   Provided by publisher.

Identifiers: LCCN 2020037210 (print) | LCCN 2020037211 (ebook) |
      ISBN 9781684000746 (cloth) | ISBN 9781684000692 (paperback) |
      ISBN 9781684000708 (ebook)

Subjects: LCSH: Dretske, Fred I. | Knowledge, Theory of. | Perception. |
   Philosophers–United States–Biography.

Classification:
   LCC B945.D744 I54 2020 (print) | LCC B945.D744 (ebook) | DDC 121–dc23

LC record available at `https://lccn.loc.gov/2020037210`

LC ebook record available at https://lccn.loc.gov/2020037211

Cover image copyright 2020 Rachel A. Skokowski

CIP

CSLI Publications is located on the campus of Stanford University.

Visit our web site at
`http://cslipublications.stanford.edu/`
for comments on this and other titles, as well as for changes
and corrections by the author and publisher.

For Paula, Rachel, and Christopher

Contents

Contributors

FRED ADAMS: Department of Linguistics and Cognitive Science, University of Delaware, Newark, DE 19716, USA.
fa@udel.edu

JOHN BARKER: Department of Philosophy, University of Illinois Springfield, Springfield, IL 62703, USA.
jbark3@uis.edu

JOHN PERRY: Department of Philosophy, Stanford University, Stanford, CA 94305, USA.
john@csli.stanford.edu

PAUL SKOKOWSKI: St. Edmund Hall, Oxford University, Oxford, 0X1 4AR, UK, and Symbolic Systems, Stanford University, Stanford, CA 94305, USA.
paulsko@stanford.edu

DENNIS STAMPE: Department of Philosophy, University of Wisconsin Madison, Madison, WI 53706, USA.
dennisstampe@earthlink.net

Acknowledgements

I would like to thank the very generous sponsors for the original conference held at Stanford in May 2015 which served as the genesis for this volume. These sponsors include the Stanford Humanities Center, the Stanford Wu Tsai Neurosciences Institute, the Center for the Study of Language and Information, John and Claire Radway, the Stanford Philosophy Department, the Stanford Humanities Dean's Office, the Stanford Office of the Provost, and the Center for the Explanation of Consciousness. I would like to thank Krista Lawlor as Chair of the Stanford Philosophy Department for her support as the volume has been put together. Dikran Karagueuzian has been invaluable, from the initial discussions to patiently shepherding the project at every stage along the way. I am also indebted to Judith Dretske, both as a friend, and as a source of various puzzle pieces that were needed to put the volume together. I should also like to thank the contributors to this volume not only for their contributions, but also their patience during the process. For comments, advice, and encouragement at random intervals, I would like to thank John Perry and Reed Guy, true friends and colleagues. Evelyn McMillan kindly provided a photo of Fred from the Stanford Philosophy archive. Thanks are also due Benjamin Przybocki for help with editing the final draft. Finally, thanks to Fred Dretske, who, as a philosopher and colleague, was the inspiration for all this.

1

Introduction

PAUL SKOKOWSKI

The papers in this volume examine several topics that Fred Dretske addressed in his philosophical career. These papers range from one of the earliest problems Fred addressed, the nature of seeing an object, to epistemological issues that Fred worked on from mid-career onwards, to issues he focused on later in his career, including information, mental representation, and conscious experience.

The idea for the volume had its genesis at a conference held by the Center for the Explanation of Consciousness at Stanford in 2015 to celebrate Fred's life and philosophical work. The conference brought together a faculty member and an ex-graduate student from the two institutions where Fred had taught before his retirement: Wisconsin and Stanford. Representing Wisconsin were Dennis Stampe as fellow faculty member and Fred Adams as an ex-PhD student. Representing Stanford were John Perry as fellow faculty member, and myself, as Fred's first PhD student at 'The Farm'. The papers in this volume were inspired by the talks given at that conference.

In addition to the papers from the conference, this volume also contains anecdotes from the participants, describing personal interactions with Fred that transformed their philosophical views on a topic, or changed their trajectory in the profession in some way. A bibliography of Fred Dretske's publications is also provided in an appendix.

Information and Mind: The Philosophy of Fred Dretske.
Paul Skokowski (ed.).
Copyright © 2020, CSLI Publications.

Fred Dretske studied Electrical Engineering at Purdue University, where he graduated with a BSEE in 1954. He then served in the military for two years before starting graduate studies in Philosophy at the University of Minnesota in 1956 under the GI Bill. He received an MA in 1958 and a PhD, with a minor in mathematics, in 1960 from the University of Minnesota. His PhD advisor at Minnesota was May Brodbeck.

Fred was a genuinely humble person, an incredibly conscientious philosopher, and an exceptionally clear writer who made otherwise very difficult concepts understandable with numerous examples. Here, his background in electrical engineering served him extremely well, in particular providing him with lucid descriptions of gauges and other measuring instruments and their capacities to provide information, functional roles, and representations in varied contexts. In my opinion, it was exactly these sorts of examples which set Fred apart from other philosophers of mind, and which made his views on information, representation, and even consciousness, so compelling and influential.

The first paper, by Fred Adams and John Barker, "Dretskean Externalism about Knowledge," examines epistemological issues surrounding Gettier-type problems that Fred first put forward in his 1971 paper "Conclusive Reasons." The second paper, by John Perry, "Representation and Possibility," compares possibilities for worlds with Dretskean-style representations with other forms of representation. The third paper, by Paul Skokowski, "Three Dogmas of Internalism," argues that the three most famous challenges to materialist theories of conscious experience are limited in their scope by applying only to internalist versions of materialism, and that externalist theories, including Dretskean ones, avoid their force. The final paper, by Dennis Stampe, "Perceptual Activity and the Object of Perception," returns to the first (and the last) philosophical topic he ever discussed with Fred—viz., which object is the cause of an impression—and develops the notion of perceptual activity and its role in explaining the nature of sensation. A brief summary of each of these papers is given immediately below. The chapters that follow contain the papers themselves, each with concluding personal anecdotes of Fred Dretske.

The first essay in the volume—Fred Adams and John Barker's paper "Dretskean Externalism about Knowledge"—deals with Dretskean themes in the theory of knowledge, in particular examining an analysis of knowledge put forward by Dretske in his 1971 paper "Conclusive Reasons." (*Dretske* 1971, p. 1-22) Adams and Barker ask what the requirements are for a true belief to count as knowledge, and by examining this question in detail throughout the paper—including contrasting the traditionalist Justified-True-Belief analysis with Gettier's challenges, and with Dretske's own analysis—

they proceed to formulate new distinctions for different varieties of knowledge.

The authors set out to defend what they call the **Conclusive Reasons Analysis of Knowing**, developed by Dretske in his 1971 paper. According to this Conclusive Reasons Analysis,

> S *knows* that p iff: (i) p is true; (ii) S believes that p; and (iii) S's believing that p is based on reasons, R, that are *conclusive*, i.e., R is such that if p weren't the case, then R wouldn't be the case.

Adams and Barker further maintain that, by excluding justification as a requirement for knowledge, the Conclusive Reasons analysis actually validates *knowledge-closure*, "the highly plausible thesis that correct inferences from known premises invariably yield knowledge of the conclusions." (p. 2, below) They contrast *knowledge-closure* with *justification-closure*, attributed to Gettier and others, that "If S is justified in believing that p and that p implies q, then if S correctly infers that q from the premises that p and p implies q, S is justified in believing that q," and argue that *justification-closure* leads to radical skepticism about knowledge (the latter argument is given in more detail towards the end of the paper). What is ironic about all this, as the authors explain, is that knowledge-closure was rejected by Dretske, and furthermore, the traditionalists generally criticized him for this rejection. Adams and Barker argue that Dretske underestimated the scope of his own Conclusive Reasons analysis, while the traditionalists overestimated their own theories, which sets the stage for the remainder of the essay.

Adams and Barker use Chisholm as an example for explaining traditional approaches to justification. They argue for three aspects of justification for the traditionalist: that beliefs be supported by reasons, that an agent's justification for a belief is available to internal reflection, and that justification is defeasible—that is, a belief's justification "can be undermined by acquisition of certain additional beliefs or experiences." (p 5, below) Such traditional accounts are internalist in nature, they argue, since internal reflection is an important aspect of justification for such accounts. These accounts are then contrasted with externalist accounts, which maintain that reflection alone is not enough to warrant believing that p. One example of externalism, attributed to F.P. Ramsey and Alvin Goldman, is called *radical warrant-externalism*. Radical warrant-externalism is supported by what Adams and Barker call the **Reliable True Belief** analysis of knowing:

S knows that p iff: (i) p is true, (ii) S believes that p, (iii) S's belief is *reliable*, i.e., the belief is produced by processes that have a high probability of yielding true beliefs; and (iv) S's believing that p is based on reasons, R, that reliably indicate that p is the case, i.e., given R, it is highly probable that p is the case.

The problem with an analysis like the above, however (as supported by a quote from Dretske in the essay), is that probabilities of less than 1 cannot be *conclusive* reasons for holding a belief. Several examples are given to support this conclusion. The upshot is that, for an externalist, the proper solution is to use *facts* instead of probabilities for a basis of qualifying a belief as knowledge. This move shows the efficacy of a mind-world connection: an agent possessing reasons that are *facts* for knowledge confers the ability to perform fact-grounded actions, thus providing a natural function for knowledge. Having the capability for fact-grounded actions provides a new Value-Enhancing Property (VEP) for beliefs, where a "VEP of a belief is a property that enhances the epistemic value of the belief." (p. 17, below)

The paper next examines the Conclusive Reasons analysis (Dretske's formulation for an agent having conclusive reasons for believing p) and considers different varieties of knowledge. A Dretskean-style argument is provided to show that perceptions and sensations can function as reasons upon which beliefs can be based. Such reasons provide the conditions for what Adams and Barker call "generic knowledge"—a variety of knowledge that, although not certain (the latter being a difficult variety of knowledge to attain in any case), is conclusive and widespread. Generic knowledge is available not only to normal adults, but also to young children and individuals with certain impairments. As hinted at earlier in the paper, an argument is now given to show how the Conclusive Reasons analysis actually implies Knowledge Closure, allowing wider acceptance of the Conclusive Reasons view.

Adams and Barker conclude with a detailed analysis of how different Value-Enhancing Properties provide conditions for different species of knowledge. These species include *tenable* knowledge, *certain* knowledge, *critical* knowledge, *contrastive* knowledge, and *generic* knowledge. The conclusive reasons VEP is seen to be special for its support of generic knowledge, by underwriting the ability for actions that are grounded in facts. Generic knowledge should therefore prove to be of particular interest to epistemologists going forward.

John Perry's essay "Representation and Possibility" considers what possibilities there could be in a world with representation. He makes a distinction between three kinds of possibilities, which he calls Dretskean possibilities, God's possibilities, and Human possibilities. In the essay, Perry makes connections between Dretske's theory of representation, as laid out in

Naturalizing the Mind, possible worlds theories, and Frege's theory of circumstance, as developed in his *Begriffsschrift*.

Dretske's theory of representation is a way of describing how systems harness information, according to Perry, where the harnessing encompasses "detection, application and goal." (p. 39, below) Sensors detect information in a lawlike way, and, when hooked up so that they have a function for the system in question, cause changes in the system. This detection and the output caused promote a goal which makes sense for the system. For instruments such as speedometers, it's usually a person who harnesses the information of the instrument, and acts upon it to further one of her goals. For example, observing a speedometer causes a driver to speed up or slow down, depending on her most recent sighting (detection) of a speed-limit sign.

Perry next points out that all this is well and good, but there are further parameters at play when we discuss the actions of a system, or the utterances of a speaker: namely, unarticulated constituents. Using one of Dretske's favorite examples, that of a magnetosome, Perry points out that a theorist articulates the parameters at work (both current and historical) in order to describe how the simple organism accomplishes its task of swimming towards oxygen-depleted water by use of detecting magnetic north. But of course, to the magnetosome, none of this matters. It simply aligns and 'swims', with no need to articulate anything whatsoever. In linguistic discourse, however, articulation becomes important, such as when speakers in different time zones decide when to next meet, or when one considers the meaning of the utterance 'It's noon'. Here, unarticulated constituents—such as places and time zones —become crucial to understanding the meanings of the times for appointments, and understanding the meanings of such simple declarations. The lesson here is that in order to harness information to accomplish goals such as making appointments, or understanding utterances of times, we often need to articulate many constituents that are left out of simple descriptions and statements.

This lesson is carried over to Dretske's theory of representation. The idea is that Dretske's model of harnessing information by acquiring a function of indication and thereby producing action, itself depends on background conditions—what John Mackie has referred to as "INUS conditions", where INUS stands for: Insufficient but Non-redundant parts of Unnecessary but Sufficient conditions. (Mackie, 1974) Dretske focused on external properties which, by being detected, cause an internal state in the system. This internal state has a function to indicate that external property (type), and this function confers the ability to cause action for the system. But in order for this to actually all work out, other background/INUS conditions need to be in place, where these background conditions were actually installed into the system at some point in order for the system to behave the way it does under those informational conditions. Perry gives several examples where self-knowledge is shown to be one of those background conditions that appear to be built in to organisms, including chickens, chimps, and humans.

Perry now compares the three kinds of possibilities for representation. The first, *Dretskean possibilities*, require only what Perry calls 'first-level circumstances,' which consists of objects, their properties, and their relations. This will work well to describe fairly low-level systems, animals such as chickens for example. Such systems can behave adequately with unarticulated constituents, and won't require concrete objects in their ontology. This is contrasted with *God's possibilities*. For example, God's plans for creating the world include: "higher-level circumstances, involving properties being instantiated by lower-level properties, quantifying over the individuals that do the ultimate instantiating." (Perry p. 47, below) Finally, Perry considers Human possibilities. This category utilizes a mixture of low-level and higher-level circumstances, with a domain of objects that are relevant to the situation that an agent finds herself in at any particular time. Perry argues that this is the right level for accommodating our concepts of information and communication.

The essay concludes by arguing that this view of possibilities leads to a rejection of the possible worlds analysis of properties as functions from worlds to extensions. Instead, we should recognize that "properties are a much more basic and intelligible part of life, animal or human, than functions from possible worlds to extensions." This was a view that Dretske emphasized. Understanding properties and their causal roles is fundamental to understanding how information is harnessed, leading to a better understanding of representation and action.

Paul Skokowski's essay "Three Dogmas of Internalism" considers three historically major challenges to materialism about the mind— Nagel's what-it-is-like argument, Kripke's modal argument, and Jackson's knowledge argument—and argues that the prevailing view that these arguments are successful against materialism amounts to no more than a dogma, for whatever force they have applies only to internalist formulations of materialism, while missing the mark entirely against externalist formulations of materialism such as Dretske's.

The first dogma is Nagel's 'what-it-is-like' arguments. An immediate problem with Nagel's 'what-it-is-like' terminology, Skokowski explains, is that there are actually three distinct ways in which 'what-it-is-like' is used. The first appears to be the way that a mental state token is part of a mental economy of such states. What-it-is-like to have that state, then, depends not just on that state, but also on relations that state has with the other states in the mental economy. The second way Nagel uses the term has to do with point of view. Nagel claims that subjective phenomena have a single point of view, and that an objective discipline such as science must seem to avoid any such views. The third way he uses the term has to do with qualia, or the subjective characters of our experiences. Skokowski points out that it is this third issue—the problem of qualia—which is now considered to comprise the hard problem of consciousness. The problem of qualia, then, is the notion of what-it-is-like worth focusing on.

Though these arguments seem to pose problems for materialism, Nagel himself does not claim that they are fatal to the materialist project. But be that as it may, Skokowski argues that Nagel's arguments are ultimately aimed only at internalist conceptions of materialism. The only externalist formulation considered—functionalism—is claimed by Nagel to be neobehaviorist, and so is dismissed out of hand. This means that the force of Nagel's what-it-is-like arguments are directed at challenging materialism to provide an internalist account of qualia. Nagel's argument therefore completely misses any externalist account of materialism. Externalist accounts of materialism are developed and defended in the remaining sections of the essay.

The next dogma to be considered is Kripke's modal argument. Skokowski shows how Kripke uses the modal argument to argue against the identity theory. Ultimately, Kripke concludes that the identity theory fails to establish that mental states are brain states, or specifically, that pains are particular brain states, such as C-fiber firings. The essay argues that Kripke's argument is not actually an argument against all kinds of materialism. Since the identity theory is an internalist theory, where mental properties are properties of internal brain states, this completely ignores externalist accounts of mental phenomena, such as Dretske's. Skokowski then proceeds to develop an externalist materialist theory. This theory uses Kripke's own example of sensing heat to show how this externalist formulation not only provides a purely materialist account of sensation, but does it through applying the very techniques Kripke has provided.

The final dogma to be considered is Jackson's knowledge argument, which gives the famous example of the brilliant neuroscientist Mary, who is kept in a black and white room. Once again, as with the what-it-is-like and the modal arguments, it turns out that the knowledge argument is only aimed at internalist versions of mind. Skokowski points out that the knowledge argument actually depends on a hidden premise, which is that Mary can *have* all the physical knowledge while being confined to her room. This premise is challenged by externalist, physical conceptions of sensation and knowledge, together with a physical account of qualia, which taken together, are shown to ultimately support the position that Mary learns something new when she exits her room. It is shown how Mary's new sensations, and knowledge, involve transactions with external physical properties that hitherto had been denied to her by her confinement.

The essay concludes with two points. The first answers Nagel's earlier dismissal of all forms of functionalism as neobehaviorist—in particular leaving out qualia in functionalist accounts of experience. Skokowski argues that externalism actually provides a form of functionalism that includes qualia as an essential component in accounting for experience—a point missed even by previous functionalists. The second point reviews how the three major arguments against materialism given by Nagel, Kripke and Jackson have really only ever been aimed at internalist accounts of materialism. By emphasizing the force of these arguments against internalist accounts of materialism, advocacy of the arguments amounts to a dogma that is blind to their fundamental shortcoming, which is to ignore externalist accounts of materialism that actually escape their purview, and which explain mental phenomena with exactly the physical tools on offer.

Dennis Stampe's paper, "Perceptual Activity and the Object of Perception", examines the role of perceptual *activity* when determining the cause of one's sensation of *X*. Stampe starts by considering the Causal Theory of Perception, which holds that what we see, feel, taste, etc., "... is the thing that causes the visual, auditory, gustatory, tactile or olfactory sensation or impression in our minds."(p. 105, below) But yet, when we consider all the causes of the impression, we don't see, feel, taste, etc. all of them. As Stampe remarks, this is a point made by Henry Price in 1932, when Price asked why, when considering the cause of seeing a table, do we not consider light rays, or neural signals, as the cause? Or why not go even further, and say that the light bulb was the cause, or the power station powering the light bulb was the cause, and so forth?

Stampe suggests that the Causal Theory needs to provide a careful conceptual analysis of all the causal processes from the object perceived all the way to the percept. But this will not do. Stampe reminds us of an objection given by Dretske to this line of reasoning in *Seeing and Knowing*. Requiring such an analysis to find the object of perception would seem to require that one would need to already understand the physical principles involved in the causal processes of perception. And this would seem to imply that before such principles were understood, no person "knew the meaning of the verb 'to see.'"

Stampe then considers a proposal to determining the cause of a percept, given later by Dretske in *Knowledge and the Flow of Information*. Here Dretske argued that a percept carried *information* about the object perceived. Information in this way picks out the object of perception. But if this is the case, why isn't the percept also, or instead, carrying information about other proximal causes of it? Like the state of the retina, for example, when one has a visual experience? Dretske's response was that the sensed object exhibited perceptual constancy, whereas the intermediary processes (retinal states, neural firings, etc.) were variable, so the intermediate states did not carry information in the right way. Instead we 'see through' these variable intermediate states until reaching the constant object of perception.

Stampe sets about to consider another factor in determining whether the thing we see is a (or the) cause of our percept. This factor is the perceptual activity of the perceiver, which includes acts done to those objects which are actually perceived. Stampe puts the claim simply: "Which one of the many causes of our visual impressions of this table is the one that we are *seeing*? How about this? It's the one we *are looking* at." (p. 111, below) This 'looking' is a behavior—a perceptual act of the observer—and moreover, "... looking at a thing is a cause of one's having a visual percept or impression— indeed an impression *of* the very thing *at* which one is looking." When looking at a table we don't see our retinal activity nor the source of the light falling on the table, etc., and Stampe points out that we are also not looking at those things, and not seeing them—but we *are looking* at the table and *seeing* the table.

In his analysis of invoking perceptual activity as a factor for determining the object of perception, Stampe wishes to avoid circularity. It's important, he stresses, that this activity not be understood to be some sort of *attempt* to perceive an object or thing. So intention is not necessary for such acts. As Stampe explains, "... the action of feeling a thing must be understood as if it were a merely physical act, *e.g.* of touching, or being touched by, or one physical body being run across the surface of another." (p. 115, below)

Why hasn't perceptual activity been considered before now as being important in determining the cause of a perception? Stampe suggests that the way the question has been traditionally put is clearly a factor: "Which of the many causes of our perceptual impression is *the object that we perceive*?" This question straightforwardly leaves out other possible causes that are not the object of impression. It is proposed instead to consider how the purported cause is itself caused to cause the percept in question, and how that might transpire. So Stampe suggests a better version of the question, "Which member of the set of causes of the impression causes the impression in such a way that *some* member of that set is thereby identified as (or constituted) the object perceived." (p. 118, below)

Stampe ends by considering non-contact modalities, such as smells, or seeing a star. In such cases, one does not directly perceive the object in question, but rather, some effusive property from it. Does perceptual action help determine the perceptual object in such cases? Stampe answers in the affirmative, but only when the causal capacity of a perceptual act has an asymmetric dependence with an intermediate cause between the object and the observer. In my reading of Stampe's argument here, the perceptual act serves as a kind of INUS condition (again, see Mackie, 1974) which provides the background requirement for determining the object of perception.

References

Dretske, F. 1971. Conclusive Reasons. *Australasian Journal of Philosophy* 49:1-22.

Dretske, F. 1981. *Knowledge and the Flow of Information*. Cambridge, MA: MIT Press.

Mackie, J. 1974. *The Cement of the Universe: A Study of Causation*. Oxford: Oxford University Press.

2

Dretskean Externalism about Knowledge

FRED ADAMS AND JOHN A. BARKER

Introduction

What requirements must be met in order for a true belief to qualify as knowledge? Myriad answers to this classic question have been proffered since Edmund Gettier dropped his bombshell on the traditional Justified-True-Belief analysis of knowing.[1] Fred Dretske's answer stands out as refreshingly simple, intuitively appealing, and, as we hope to show, unusually resistant to refutation. According to Dretske, a true belief qualifies as knowledge if and only if it is based on *conclusive reasons*, that is, on reasons that wouldn't obtain unless the belief were true.[2] Although many contemporary theorists assume that analyses like Dretske's have been discredited, we have argued in a series of recent papers that such accounts are alive and well.[3]

---

[1] Gettier 1963. See Shope 1983 for a survey of attempts to analyze knowledge during the first post-Gettier decade, and Ichikawa and Steup 2017 for a recent survey of such attempts.

[2] This is a rough formulation of the analysis proffered in Dretske 1971, an analysis that is quoted verbatim and discussed at length later in the paper. Treatment of ways in which this analysis was modified in Dretske's later writings is beyond the scope of this paper; for discussion of such modifications, see, e.g., Adams 1986, 2004, 2011, and 2014.

[3] See Adams 2011 and 2014; Adams and Clarke 2005, 2016a and 2016b; Adams, Barker, and Clarke 2016, 2017, and 2018; Adams, Barker, and Figurelli 2012, and Barker and Adams 2010 and 2012.

Information and Mind: The Philosophy of Fred Dretske.
Paul Skokowski (ed.).
Copyright © 2020, CSLI Publications.

In this paper we defend the following Dretske-style analysis:

Conclusive Reasons Analysis of Knowing (ConclusiveReasonsAK):
S *knows* that p iff: (i) p is true; (ii) S believes that p; and (iii) S's believing that p is based on reasons, R, that are *conclusive*, i.e., R is such that if p weren't the case, then R wouldn't be the case.[4, 5]

One of our principal aims is to show that this account accords with many of the most intuitively appealing features of the traditional analysis, especially regarding the central role that *reasons for believing* play in knowledge acquisition. An even more important aim, however, is to establish that ConclusiveReasonsAK, owing partly to its excluding justification as a requirement for knowledge, validates *knowledge-closure*, the highly plausible thesis that correct inferences from known premises invariably yield knowledge of the conclusions:

KnowledgeClosure: If S knows that p and that p implies q, then if S correctly infers that q from the premises that p and p implies q, S knows that q.[6]

We argue that the corresponding *justification-closure* thesis that Gettier and many other theorists have accepted,

---

[4]We refer to ConclusiveReasonsAK as a *Dretske-style* analysis because it differs somewhat from Dretske's own analysis. Our analysis employs a subjunctive conditional of the form 'if p weren't the case, then R wouldn't be the case', which is to be construed as a *relevant conditional* whose truth-conditions are formally codified in the paradox-free System R of Relevant Implication; see, e.g., Belnap 1967, Barker 1969, Bacon 1971, Anderson and Belnap 1975, Anderson, Belnap, and Dunn 1992, Mares 2004, and Adams, Barker, and Clarke 2017. As we argue in the latter paper, use of a relevant conditional, among other benefits, enables our analysis to accommodate knowledge of necessary truths. Our analysis employs a separate thesis, EpistemicBasing, to characterize the basing relation, which Dretske characterized within the formulation of his analysis.

[5]We use 'p is true' in the sense of 'it is true that p'; similar departures from strict grammatical form are used throughout the paper. In keeping with widely accepted practice, we refer to ConclusiveReasonsAK and its competitors as *analyses* of knowing, as they purport to specify "necessary and sufficient conditions for knowing that something is so without making use of the term 'know' itself or a cognate term." (Hyman 2006, p. 908) See Williamson 2000 for a significantly different conception of such analyses, and for arguments against quests for analyses so conceived. We make no attempt to formulate conditions of knowing that are independent of each other, as we think such attempts are misguided—in Dretskean analyses, for instance, the truth condition is implied by the other conditions.

[6]Several different formulations of knowledge-closure have been discussed in the epistemological literature. This formulation is preferable for present purposes.

JustificationClosure: If S is justified in believing that p and that p implies q, then if S correctly infers that q from the premises that p and p implies q, S is justified in believing that q.

is fundamentally counterintuitive and fuels radical skepticism about knowledge. This development is distinctly ironic. Dretske himself rejected knowledge-closure, and argued that his analysis entailed its falsity.[7] Many traditionalists decried his rejection of knowledge-closure, contending that any analysis that clashed with this closure principle was *ipso facto* unacceptable. For example, Lawrence BonJour considered rejection of the principle a *reductio ad absurdum* of analyses that entail its falsity, and Richard Feldman commented: "...the idea that this principle is false strikes me, and many other philosophers, as one of the least plausible ideas to come down the philosophical pike in recent years."[8] We attempt to show that Dretske underestimated the capabilities of his theory, and that traditionalists overestimated the capabilities of theirs.

1 Knowledge and Justification

Gettier's formulation of the traditional analysis employed an undefined notion of epistemic justification: "S knows that P IFF (i.e., if and only if) (i) P is true, (ii) S believes that P, and (iii) S is justified in believing that P."[9] Many debates regarding the merits of this analysis have centered on the question of precisely what is involved in being justified in believing a proposition.[10] Gettier provided clues regarding his intent by citing Roderick Chisholm's view that S must have "adequate evidence" for p, and A. J. Ayer's view that S must have "the right to be sure" that p is true.[11] BonJour has characterized the traditional conception of knowledge in a way that casts additional light on the appropriate notion of justification:

---

[7]See, e.g., Dretske 1971 and 2005.

[8]BonJour 1987, pp. 310 ff. and Feldman 1994, p. 1.

[9]Gettier 1963, p. 121.

[10]We do not presuppose that S's being justified in believing a proposition involves either: (a) S's being able to *justify* believing the proposition, or (b) S's being able to *establish* that she is justified in believing the proposition, or even (c) S's being able to *think* that she is justified in believing the proposition. Relationships between S's being justified in believing a proposition and S's possessing various propositional attitudes regarding this state of affairs will be discussed later in the paper.

[11]Chisholm 1957, p. 16; and Ayer 1956, p. 34. Gettier also noted that "Plato seems to be considering some such definition at *Theaetetus* 201, and perhaps accepting one at *Meno* 98." (p. 121, Note 1)

Perhaps the most pervasive conviction within the Western epistemological tradition is that in order for a person's belief to constitute *knowledge* it is necessary (though not sufficient) that it be justified or warranted or rationally grounded, that the person have an adequate *reason* for accepting it.[12]

In view of these considerations, we'll focus on a formulation of the traditional analysis that facilitates comparison with ConclusiveReasonsAK and highlights the key role played by reasons for believing:

JustifiedTrueBeliefAK: S knows that p iff: (i) p is true; (ii) S believes that p, and (iii) S's believing that p is based on reasons, R, that make S justified in believing that p.[13]

2 Reasons, Accessibility, and Defeasibility

How is the traditional notion of justification to be explicated? According to Chisholm, a leading 20th century traditionalist, "The term 'justify', in its application to a belief, is a term of epistemic appraisal—a term that is used to say something about the reasonableness of belief."[14] There are three important aspects of traditional conceptualizations of epistemic justification that a satisfactory explication should attempt to accommodate. The first is the above-mentioned association with *reasons for believing*. The second is the widely-shared presupposition that S's being justified in believing that p is an *internal* state of S, that is, a state that is normally accessible to S via reflection. Roughly speaking, if S is justified in believing that p, she can normally determine via reflection that she is so justified. For present purposes *internalism*, A.K.A. *accessibilism*, can be construed as the view that one or more of the conditions associated with a true belief's qualifying as knowledge is normally accessible to the subject via reflection.[15] For instance, internalism about justification is the view that S's being justified in believing that p is a state of S that is reflectively accessible to S; and internalism about reasons for believing that p is the view that S's believing that p on the basis of certain reasons is a state of S that is reflectively accessible to S. Such reflective accessibility would be of considerable epistemic value, for it would facilitate the subject's engaging in metacognitive self-monitoring and in rational

---

[12] BonJour 1998, p. 1.

[13] Throughout this paper we use the expression 'S is justified in believing that p' in a way that implies that S *justifiedly believes* that p rather than merely that S is in a position to do so. Hence, the truth of Clause (iii) presupposes the truth of Clause (ii).

[14] Chisholm 1977, p. 6.

[15] *Accessibilism* is to be distinguished from *mentalism*, the view that what ultimately makes a believer justified in believing a proposition consists in some mental state of the believer. Although the two views are related in complex ways, they are distinct views, and acceptance of one doesn't entail acceptance of the other. Treatment of mentalism is beyond the scope of this paper.

deliberation about whether to initiate, to continue, or to terminate inquiry and investigative procedures regarding propositions of interest.[16] (Chisholm even linked justification to *knowledge of knowledge*: "...the things we know are justified for us in the following sense: we can know what it is, on any occasion, that constitutes our grounds, or reason, or evidence for thinking that we know.")[17]

The third important aspect of traditional conceptualizations of justification is the *defeasibility* of justification—the justificational status of a belief can be undermined by acquisition of certain additional beliefs or experiences.[18] To illustrate, suppose that during a visit to London Zoo, Sue justifiedly believed that the animal she saw in the zebra enclosure was a zebra on the basis of its appearing to her to be one. Suppose she then acquired a belief that several zonkeys (zebra-donkey hybrids) that looked like zebras were in the same enclosure.[19] It's plausible that, *ceteris paribus*, Sue was no longer justified in believing that the animal she saw was a zebra on the basis of her visual experience.

Accordingly, we seek to explicate epistemic justification in a way that accommodates its linkage to reasons for believing, to reflective accessibility, and to defeasibility. To accomplish this, we'll seek guidance from Chisholm's discussions of justification—as Matthias Steup has noted, "Access internalism has been defended by Roderick Chisholm, who can reasonably be viewed as the chief advocate of internalist, traditional epistemology in the second half of the twentieth century."[20] Drawing inspiration from Chisholm's astute reflections, we proffer the following explication:

---

[16]For recent research findings regarding the significance of a subject's cognitive access to her own perceptual experiences, see Travers, Frith and Shea 2017.

[17]Chisholm 1966, p. 17. The association with knowledge of knowledge is quite understandable with respect to theorists who endorse JustifiedTrueBeliefAK. Assume for the sake of argument that this analysis is correct. Now suppose that p is true, that S believes that p, and that S is justified in believing that p; suppose also that S competently reflects on her cognitive situation regarding p. It seems plausible that each of the following will then obtain: p is true, S believes that p, S is justified in believing that p, and therefore S knows that p; S believes that S believes that p, S believes that S is justified in believing that p, S is justified in believing that S believes that p, S is justified in believing that S is justified in believing that p, and therefore S knows that S knows that p.

[18]See, e.g., Lehrer and Paxson 1969, Klein 1971, Swain 1974, and Barker 1976.

[19]Charles Darwin recounted that a triple hybrid, from a bay mare and a hybrid from a male ass and a female zebra, was once shown at London Zoo; see, e.g., http://www.ebooklibrary.org/articles/zonkey). For an informative video about zonkeys, see, e.g., https://www.youtube.com/watch?v=1gstrZIK-2I.

[20]Steup 2017, Note 21.

EpistemicJustification: S is *justified in believing* that p iff S's believing that p is based on reasons that make believing that p more reasonable from S's perspective than suspending judgment regarding p.[21]

In light of this explication, it's plausible that when S is justified in believing that p, S is normally in a position to determine via reflection that she is so justified—if S is justified in believing that p, then if she were to consider whether believing that p is more reasonable from her perspective than suspending judgment regarding p, she could determine that it is the more reasonable thing to do. Thus, EpistemicJustification grounds the following plausible thesis:

JustificationInternalism: If S is justified in believing that p, then she could normally determine via reflection that she is justified in believing that p; in other words, if S is justified in believing that p, then if she understood what is involved in being justified in believing that p, and reflected on whether she is justified in believing that p, she could, *ceteris paribus*, determine that she is justified in believing that p.[22]

---

[21] Cf. Chisholm 1977, p. 7, where the property of *being beyond reasonable doubt for a subject* is explicated along similar lines. It's plausible that this level of epistemic warrantedness is appropriate for the doxastic attitude associated with knowledge, which Dretske characterized as "... S believes, without doubt, reservation, or question, that P is the case..." (Dretske 1971, p. 12). Following Chisholm's lead, we treat comparative reasonableness as a primitive notion, which we take to concern attaining what can be called the *natural goal* of belief regarding a proposition, viz. the goal of possessing the belief if and only if the proposition were to be true. Accordingly, believing that p is more reasonable from S's perspective than suspending judgment regarding p just in case, relative to S's perspective (i.e., S's past and present experiences, S's fund of beliefs, S's perceptual and intellectual capabilities and powers, etc.), believing that p is preferable to suspending judgment regarding p for purposes of promoting attainment of the natural goal of belief regarding p. This construal of comparative reasonableness is similar to Chisholm's: "We may assume that every person is subject to a purely intellectual requirement: that of trying his best to bring it about that for any proposition p he considers, he accepts p if and only if p is true... One might say that this is the person's responsibility or duty qua intellectual being.... One way, then, of re-expressing the locution 'p is more reasonable than q for S at t' is to say this: 'S is so situated at t that his intellectual requirement, his responsibility as an intellectual being, is better fulfilled by p than by q'." (Chisholm 1977, p. 14).

[22] The 'normally' and 'ceteris paribus' qualifiers are meant to allow for cases in which S is unable to determine that she is justified in believing that p owing to intellectual immaturity, cognitive impairment, lack of the relevant concepts, insufficient time or interest, etc. (For present purposes, 'S could determine that __' can be construed simply as 'S could acquire a non-accidentally true belief that __').

Accordingly, our Chisholm-inspired explication of justification succeeds in supporting internalism about justification.[23]

When S is justified in believing that p, it is *normally* the case that she can access this state of affairs via reflection. Nevertheless, it is possible for S to be justified in believing that p even if she lacks the wherewithal to access her own mental states. To illustrate, suppose that Annie is a young child who sees an animal, X, and justifiedly believes it to be a cat on the basis of its appearing to her that this is the case. EpistemicJustification implies that believing that X is a cat is more reasonable from her perspective than suspending judgment regarding the matter; and JustificationInternalism implies that if she understood what is involved in being justified in believing that X is a cat, and reflected on whether believing that X is a cat is more reasonable from her perspective than suspending judgment regarding it, she could, *ceteris paribus*, determine that believing it is the more reasonable thing to do. It does not follow, however, that she is actually capable of determining that this is the case. Even if she is afflicted with severe autism and will never develop such a capability, it is still the case that she is justified in believing that X is a cat.[24]

EpistemicJustification can account for phenomena associated with the defeasibility of justification. For example, suppose that when Sue saw the zebra, it was more reasonable from her perspective for her to believe that what she saw was a zebra on the basis of her visual experience than to suspend judgment on the matter. Upon acquiring a belief that there were zebra-lookalikes in the vicinity, however, it became more reasonable from her perspective for her to suspend judgment regarding whether what she saw was a zebra. Thus, EpistemicJustification can capture intuitions associated with the defeasibility of justification as well as intuitions associated with its reflective accessibility.[25]

---

[23] Some contemporary theorists use the term 'justified' and its cognates in a radically different sense, a sense in which S can be "justified" in believing a proposition even if the belief isn't based on reasons for believing but is merely a product of truth-conducive processes. EpistemicJustification and JustificationInternalism are not concerned with being "justified" in such a sense of the term, which has no intrinsic relationship to the reasonableness of belief from the subject's perspective. We will comment on this matter later in the paper.

[24] For discussion of reflective access disabilities associated with autism, see, e.g., Gordon and Barker 1994, Baron-Cohen 1995, and Barker 2002.

[25] According to JustifiedTrueBeliefAK, justification has the function of enabling true beliefs to qualify as knowledge. From a traditionalist perspective, it's plausible that justification, as explicated by EpistemicJustification, is necessary for knowledge and, together with true belief and possibly some additional conditions, is sufficient for knowledge. We argue, however, that justification is not necessary for knowledge itself, which we call *generic* knowledge, but only for certain *species* of knowledge, where its function is to facilitate inquiry-oriented investigative procedures. For an in-depth discussion of the function of justification, see Adams 1986.

3   Warrant-Internalism and Warrant-Externalism

We now introduce the technical expression 'S is *warranted* in believing that p' to denote the situation in which S satisfies each one of the conditions, whatever they are, that are required in order for her true belief that p to constitute knowledge. (Accordingly, it is "true by definition" that S knows that p if and only if p is true, S believes that p, and S is warranted in believing that p.)   Theorists who accept both EpistemicJustification and Justified-TrueBeliefAK would find the following thesis acceptable:

> **WarrantInternalism**: If S is warranted in believing that p, then she could normally determine via reflection that she is warranted in believing that p; in other words, if S is warranted in believing that p, then if she understood what is involved in being warranted in believing that p, and she reflected on whether she is warranted in believing that p, she could, *ceteris paribus,* determine that she is warranted in believing that p.

As we'll now argue, the opposing thesis,

> **WarrantExternalism**: If S is warranted in believing that p, it might nevertheless be the case that she couldn't normally determine via reflection that she is warranted in believing that p.

would be acceptable to almost all theorists who accept EpistemicJustification but reject JustifiedTrueBeliefAK.

We begin by distinguishing between two types of warrant-externalists: *moderates*, who hold that S can know that p only if S's believing that p is based on reasons she possesses for believing that p; and *radicals*, who hold that S can know that p even if her believing that p isn't based on such reasons. Many theorists have proffered analyses that in effect modify Justified-TrueBeliefAK by adding a fourth condition intended to handle Gettier-type counterexamples. Since the added condition is usually one whose obtaining is not reflectively accessible to the subject, such theorists are typically moderate warrant-externalists. To illustrate, consider a theorist who attempts to handle Gettier-type counterexamples by proffering the following analysis:

> **JustifiedTrueBeliefAK***: S knows that p iff: (i) p is true; (ii) S believes that p, (iii) S's believing that p is based on reasons, R, that make S justified in believing that p; and (iv) S's being justified in believing that p on the basis of R does not depend on any false premises.

Since the fact that (iv) holds wouldn't normally be reflectively accessible to S, such a theorist would constitute a moderate warrant-externalist.[26]

Similarly, theorists who accept ConclusiveReasonsAK would qualify as moderate warrant-externalists—when S believes that p on the basis of conclusive reasons, R, the fact that R wouldn't obtain if p weren't the case typically isn't something that is reflectively accessible to S. Let's now consider a traditionalist who attempts to avoid Gettier-type problems by proffering the following analysis, which incorporates a conclusive-reasons requirement as a fourth condition:

> **JustifiedTrueBeliefAK****: S knows that p iff: (i) p is true; (ii) S believes that p, (iii) S's believing that p is based on reasons, R, that make S justified in believing that p; and (iv) R is such that if p weren't the case, then R wouldn't be the case.

Such a theorist would constitute a moderate warrant-externalist, since even though Clause (iii) describes a reflectively accessible condition, Clause (iv) does not—as we noted above, the fact that R wouldn't obtain if p weren't the case typically isn't reflectively accessible to S. JustifiedTrueBeliefAK** appears to be superior to most, if not all, of its competitors, as it seems to be immune to Gettier-type counterexamples. After investigating numerous counterexamples to analyses of knowing that add a fourth, anti-Gettier condition, we have become convinced that none of them discredits this analysis. We argue later, however, that this analysis should be construed as specifying necessary and sufficient conditions for a valuable *species of knowledge* rather than for knowledge itself, which we'll call *generic knowledge*.

JustifiedTrueBeliefAK** appears to lack coherence, since Clauses (iii) and (iv) seem to have no connection to each other. The following modified analysis remedies this problem:

> **JustifiedTrueBeliefAK*****: S knows that p iff: (i) p is true; (ii) S believes that p, (iii) S's believing that p is based on reasons, R, that make S justified in believing that p; and (iv) if p weren't the case, then S wouldn't be justified in believing that p on the basis of R.

This analysis obviously exhibits coherence. And since Clause (iv) of the previous analysis entails Clause (iv) of this one, neither of these analyses actually lacks coherence.

---

[26]Incidentally, this analysis has been discredited by counterexamples; see, e.g., Shope 1983, pp. 21 ff.

The following considerations indicate that JustifiedTrueBeliefAK** and JustifiedTrueBeliefAK*** are closely related to a very influential kind of traditional analysis that centers on the plausible hypothesis that knowledge is *indefeasibly* justified true belief, that is, justified true belief that is immune to legitimate defeat.[27] We'll focus on the following version of an indefeasibly justified true belief analysis:

> **AbsolutelyJustifiedTrueBeliefAK**: S knows that p iff: (i) p is true, (ii) S believes that p, (iii) S's believing that p is based on reasons, R, that make S justified in believing that p; and (iv) S is *absolutely* justified in believing that p on the basis of R, i.e., for every true q_1 there is a true q_2 that is such that S would still be justified in believing that p on the basis of R if S were justified in believing that q_1 and q_2 and S believed that p solely on the basis of R.[28]

The following case illustrates this analysis. During a guided tour of London Zoo, Jackie saw a zebra, X, and justifiedly believed that X was a zebra on the basis of its appearing to him that this was the case. Unbeknownst to him, the tour guide, Mildred, who was a retired philosophy professor with an eccentric sense of humor, said that X was a zonkey that was a temporary replacement for a sick zebra. Mildred's saying this constituted what can be called a *menacer* of Jackie's justified belief that X was a zebra—if he had justifiedly believed she said this, his zebra belief might no longer have been justified.[29] But there was a true proposition, viz. that she was joking, that constituted what can be called a *protector* of his justified zebra belief—if he had

---

[27]For analyses of this kind, see, e.g, Lehrer and Paxson 1969, Klein 1971 and 1981, Hilpinen 1971, and Barker 1976.

[28]This analysis is an abbreviation of:

> **AbsolutelyJustifiedTrueBeliefAK**: S knows that p iff: (i) p is true, (ii) S believes that p, (iii) S's believing that p is based on reasons, R, that make S justified in believing that p; and (iv) S is *absolutely* justified in believing that p on the basis of R, i.e., for every true q_1 there is a true q_2 that is such that S would still be justified in believing that p on the basis of R if: (a) S were justified in believing that q_1 and q_2; (b) S believed that p solely on the basis of R; and (c) it remained the case that p.

The specification in Clause (iv) (b) regarding S's believing that p *solely* on the basis of R ensures that the belief's actual basis, R, isn't supplemented or replaced with information contained in q_1 or in q_2 to constitute a *different* basis for the belief. See Barker 1976 for an analysis that is substantially the same as AbsolutelyJustifiedTrueBeliefAK, and see Shope 1983, p. 73 for a counterexample to Barker's analysis that Clause (iv) (c) is designed to handle.

[29]We employ the term 'menacer' instead of the more commonly employed term 'defeater' because no defeating is occurring—in many cases a menacer merely has the *potential* to defeat a justification. (Use of the terms 'menacer' and 'protector' is not essential to the formulation of AbsolutelyJustifiedTrueBeliefAK.)

justifiedly believed not only that she said what she said, but also that she was joking, then he would have remained justified in believing that X was a zebra *solely on the same basis as before.*[30] Jackie was *absolutely* justified in believing that X was a zebra, for his justified belief was based on reasons that were such that for every menacer of the belief there was a protector that could nullify the threat of the menacer without supplying him with new or supplemented reasons for the belief.

As the following considerations show, absolutely justified true beliefs are much more valuable than mere justified true beliefs, for they are guaranteed to be based on conclusive reasons. Assume for the sake of the argument that S's believing that p on the basis of R is absolutely justified, but R isn't a conclusive reason for believing p. Let q_1 be the true proposition that R might be the case even if p weren't the case. If S justifiedly believed q_1, then the justificational status of S's believing p on the basis of R would be destroyed. S would no longer be justified in believing p on the basis of R, for it would no longer be the case that S's believing p on this basis would be more reasonable from S's perspective than suspending judgment regarding p. In other words, S's suspending judgment regarding p would be at least as reasonable from S's perspective as believing p. Furthermore, there is no true proposition q_2 that would nullify the threat stemming from q_1 without supplying S with new or supplemented reasons for believing p. Thus, given that S possesses an absolutely justified belief, it follows that S's belief is based on conclusive reasons.[31]

This result is quite significant, for it establishes that there is a deep relationship between indefeasibly justified true beliefs, on the one hand, and true beliefs that are based on conclusive reasons, on the other. Nevertheless, as we'll show later, AbsolutelyJustifiedTrueBeliefAK is inferior to ConclusiveReasonsAK as an analysis of generic knowledge—among other flaws, it is incompatible with KnowledgeClosure.

4 Reliability Analyses of Knowing

Reliable True Belief theorists like F. P. Ramsey and Alvin Goldman are to be classified as *radical* warrant-externalists, as they have proffered analyses

---

[30]The term 'solely' implies that Jackie would have been justified in believing that X was a zebra on the basis of his *original* reasons rather than on a basis that includes *different* reasons.

[31]See Klein 1981, pp. 151 ff. and Klein 2012, pp. 152 ff., for an analysis of knowing that is similar to Barker's and likewise implies that a belief qualifies as knowledge only if it is based on conclusive reasons.

of knowing that do not specify that the subject's belief must be based on reasons for believing.[32] Consider, for instance, the following reliability analysis:

ReliableTrueBeliefAK: S knows that p iff: (i) p is true, (ii) S believes that p, and (iii) S's belief is *reliable*, i.e., the belief is produced by processes that have a high probability of producing true beliefs.

As the following case shows, this analysis is subject to counterexamples precisely because it doesn't require that beliefs be reason-based in order to qualify as knowledge. Gertrude believed that she was going to fail a certain test, but her belief wasn't based on any reasons she possessed. Unbeknownst to her, there were causal processes that resulted in her believing she would fail and also resulted in her failing.[33] Although her achievements on tests of this kind in the past provided her with excellent evidence that she would ace the test, these causal processes, which only recently came into play, now reliably produce failure-beliefs and corresponding failures—when she believes that she will fail, such processes are almost invariably responsible both for the belief and for her failing. Since her belief that she would fail the test wasn't based on any reasons she possessed, it's implausible that it qualified as knowledge. Nevertheless, ReliableTrueBeliefAK has the consequence that the belief did qualify.[34]

---

[32]See, e.g., Ramsey 1931 and Goldman 1979 and 1986. For in-depth discussions of Goldman's reliabilism, see, e.g., McLaughlin 2016. Goldman, who has been a leading proponent of a reliabilist analysis of knowing and an influential opponent of traditional analyses, employed the term 'justified belief' and its cognates (in Goldman 1979 and in many later publications) in a sense broad enough to include beliefs that are produced by truth-conducive processes but aren't reason-based and have no intrinsic relationship with reflective accessibility or defeasibility. One of us (Fred Adams) once asked Goldman why he adopted this terminology, and received an answer that suggested that a primary motivation was to secure a better hearing for his reliabilist view among traditionalists. While this tactical maneuver succeeded in getting many theorists to use the terms as Goldman used them, it appears to have been strategically counterproductive, as it has given rise to considerable ambiguity and vagueness in many epistemological discussions, and has to some extent shifted attention away from conditions associated with pre-analytic notions of knowledge toward conditions associated with theory-laden notions of "justification." Such developments have even led some theorists to recommend abandoning justification terminology altogether; see, e.g., Alston 2005. Our employment of the technical expression 'S is *warranted* in believing that p' is intended to avoid expropriating the traditionalists' expression 'S is *justified* in believing that p'. See, e.g., Plantinga 1993 for a somewhat similar use of *warranted belief* terminology.

[33]The belief could even have been a "self-fulfilling" one—it could have resulted in her being depressed, and this in turn could have resulted in her failing.

[34]Cf. BonJour's critique of Goldman's reliability analysis in BonJour 1980. It should be noted that if Gertrude had learned that her failure-beliefs were repeatedly followed by her failures, she might have acquired good reasons upon which to base the beliefs.

Counterexamples of this kind could be avoided by revising the analysis along the following lines:

ReliableTrueBeliefAK*: S knows that p iff: (i) p is true, (ii) S believes that p, (iii) S's belief is *reliable*, i.e., the belief is produced by processes that have a high probability of yielding true beliefs; and (iv) S's believing that p is based on reasons, R, that reliably indicate that p is the case, i.e., given R, it is highly probable that p is the case.

This modified reliability analysis has the desirable consequence that Gertrude's belief did not qualify as knowledge, as it wasn't based on reasons for believing. Since the analysis specifies that S's belief must be reason-based, theorists who adopt it would qualify as moderates rather than as radicals. As the following considerations indicate, ReliableTrueBeliefAK* is closely related to ConclusiveReasonsAK. Clause (iv) of the analysis, "S's believing that p is based on reasons, R, that *reliably indicate* that p is the case, i.e., given R, it is highly probable that p is the case," is implied by Clause (iii) of ConclusiveReasonsAK, "S's believing that p is based on reasons, R, that are *conclusive*, i.e., R is such that if p weren't the case, then R wouldn't be the case." The subjunctive conditional in Clause (iii) of ConclusiveReasonsAK is true only if there is a nomic connection between R's being the case and p's being the case, a connection that ensures that, given the circumstances, there is a reliable relationship—indeed, an *absolutely* reliable relationship—between R's being the case and p's being the case.[35]

5   Lottery Cases

Unlike ConclusiveReasonsAK, ReliableTrueBeliefAK* is subject to counterexamples involving lottery-type situations. According to Dretske,

> If your reasons for believing P are such that you *might* have them when P is false, then they aren't good enough to *know* that P is true. You need something more. That is why you can't know you are going to lose a lottery just because your chances of losing are 99.99 percent. Even with those odds, you still might win (someone with those odds against him *will* win).[36]

Consider the following case. Tom and Dick bought tickets to an upcoming MegaMoolah lottery, having chosen "lucky" numbers in accordance with instructions provided by a popular guidebook on winning strategies. Meanwhile, Harry was given a ticket to the same lottery by an acquaintance. Each

---

[35]See, e.g., Adams, Barker, and Clarke 2017 and Barker 1969 for relevant discussions.
[36]Dretske 2005, pp. 43–44.

of the men planned to buy a new car with their winnings. Upon carefully researching their situations, they came to believe that they weren't going to win. Tom and Dick each based his belief on the fact that there was only one chance in a billion that he would win. Harry discovered that his ticket was a fake, and based his belief on this fact. Each of the men decided not to wait for the drawing and immediately bought used cars because they believed that they wouldn't win.[37] The reasons upon which all three beliefs were based were reliable indicators of the truth of the beliefs; Harry's reason, however, was also a conclusive reason for his belief. It turned out that Tom's and Harry's beliefs were true, but Dick's was false.

Did Tom, Dick or Harry know that he wasn't going to win, and did he buy a used car because he wasn't going to win? With regard to Tom and Dick, it's plausible that the answers to the questions are negative—neither of them knew that he wasn't going to win, and neither bought a used car because he wasn't going to win. With regard to Harry, however, it's plausible that the answers are affirmative—he knew that he wasn't going to win, and he bought a used car because he wasn't going to win. In all three cases the beliefs were produced by processes that had a high probability of yielding true beliefs. And in all three cases the beliefs were based on reasons that qualified as reliable indicators of the truth. Only Harry's belief, however, was based on conclusive reasons—if it had been the case that he was going to win, then it wouldn't (indeed, couldn't) have been the case that his ticket was a fake. And only Harry bought a used car because of the fact that he wasn't going to win, rather than merely because of the belief that he wasn't going to win.

Harry's buying the used car constitutes what we'll call a *fact-grounded* action, as it was performed not only because of a belief, viz. the belief that he wasn't going to win, but also because of the fact that accounted for the belief's being true, viz., the fact that he wasn't going to win. Harry's knowing that he wasn't going to win had a highly significant impact on his buying the used car—it connected the mind-state consisting of his believing that he wasn't going to win to the corresponding world-state consisting of the fact that he wasn't going to win in a way that made the world-state his reason, or one of his reasons, for performing the action, and this enabled the action to qualify as a fact-grounded one. In other words, his knowledge enabled him to do something, viz. buying the used car, because of a reason that was a *fact*, viz. the fact that he wasn't going to win, rather than merely a *belief*. Such a connection between mind and world was absent in Tom's case. Granted, the mind-state consisting of his believing that he wasn't going to win was

---

[37]Throughout this paper we use the term 'because' exclusively to refer to reasons for actions, including such "mental actions" as believing, rather than to causes or to other explanatory factors.

accompanied by the world-state consisting of the fact that he wasn't going to win. Nevertheless, owing to his belief's failing to qualify as knowledge, the world-state failed to become his reason for buying the used car—the action failed to become a fact-grounded one.

6 Fact-Grounded Action and Epistemic Value

Knowledge, it seems, empowers minds to function in a world of facts, for it makes actions explainable by facts about the world, even when such facts concern the future. Consider the following plausible theses:

> **KnowledgeEfficacy**: If S does something because S believes that p is the case, then if S knows that p is the case, S does it because p is the case; in other words, if at least one of S's reasons for doing something is that S believes that p is the case, then if S knows that p is the case, at least one of S's reasons for doing it is the fact that p is the case.[38]

> **KnowledgeInvolvement**: If S does something not only because S believes that p is the case, but also because p is the case, then S knows that p is the case; in other words, if at least one of S's reasons for doing something is that S believes that p is the case, and at least one of S's reasons for doing it is that p is the case, then S knows that p is the case.[39]

These theses together entail the following thesis:

> **KnowledgeProfusion**: If S does something because S believes that p is the case, then S does it because p is the case if and only if S knows that p is the case; in other words, if at least one of S's reasons for doing something is that S believes that p is the case, then at least one of S's reasons for doing it is the fact that p is the case if and only if S knows that p is the case.

---

[38]See Barker and Adams 2012 and Adams, Barker and Clarke 2017 for discussions of KnowledgeEfficacy. We intend for the thesis to be applicable to any action that an agent does for a reason, including not only ordinary reason-based actions but also "mental actions" such as believing, doubting, hoping, and wanting. (Cf. Hyman 2006, 2010, and 2015.)

[39]See Barker and Adams 2012 for discussion of KnowledgeInvolvement. Some theorists have endorsed a simpler thesis: If S does something because p is the case, then S knows that p is the case. For discussion and references, see Alvarez 2016. We have discussed the simpler thesis elsewhere, and have argued that it is subject to counterexamples (see Barker and Adams 2012, pp. 45 ff.).

In the *Meno* Plato discussed a key question about knowledge: Why is knowledge more valuable than mere true belief? Suppose that, as MapQuest indicates, you can drive from Athens to Larissa by taking A1. If possessing a true belief that A1 goes to Larissa would enable you to take the right road just as well as possessing knowledge, why would your belief's constituting knowledge be of any additional importance? KnowledgeEfficacy implies that your knowing that A1 goes to Larissa would enable you to take this road *because it goes to Larissa*—your taking A1 would qualify as a fact-grounded action.

According to John Hyman,

> ... if I believe, but do not know, that Larissa is due north, my reason for taking the road that leads north cannot be the fact that Larissa is due north, regardless of whether my belief is true. My reason may be that I believe that Larissa is due north, or that Larissa is probably due north, or that a sign indicates that Larissa is due north, or that someone told me that Larissa is due north. But the fact that Larissa is due north cannot be my reason, unless it is a fact I know.[40]

This indicates that Hyman would accept KnowledgeInvolvement. If KnowledgeEfficacy and KnowledgeInvolvment are both true, and hence KnowledgeProfusion is true, then knowledge has distinctive value—knowledge enables one to act for reasons that are facts, while mere true belief cannot do this. It's plausible that possessing knowledge is necessary and sufficient for possessing the ability to perform fact-grounded actions, and that providing this ability constitutes what can be called the *natural function* of knowledge.[41]

Let's say that a *Value-Enhancing Property* (*VEP*) of a belief is a property that enhances the epistemic value of the belief.[42] Among the VEPs that have been extensively explored by epistemologists are the following: (a) being true; (b) being justified; (c) being based on good evidence; (d) being based on good reasons; (e) being based on conclusive reasons; (f) being produced

---

[40]Hyman 2010, p. 412.

[41]While the thesis that knowledge has distinctive value is widely accepted, interpretations of the thesis and arguments for accepting it differ widely, and the thesis itself has been rejected by some theorists. See, e.g., Haddock, Millar, and Pritchard 2009 for discussions of the value of knowledge. As we have explained elsewhere, our view regarding the nature of knowledge closely resembles Hyman's, yet differs from his in significant ways. Roughly speaking, we hold that one's knowing that p *provides* one with the ability to do things because of the fact that p, while Hyman holds that one's knowing that p *consists in* one's having the ability to do things because of the fact that p. See Barker and Adams 2012 for discussion of Hyman's view and of objections to it.

[42]For present purposes, the epistemic value of a belief that p can be construed as its value in relation to the natural goal of belief, to the natural function of knowledge, and to the perceptual and intellectual capabilities that contribute to attaining this goal and fulfilling this function.

by reliable, truth-conducive processes; (g) being safe; and (h) being produced by the exercise of intellectual virtues.[43] Let's now augment the above case by supposing that Tom's belief that he wasn't going to win the lottery possessed every one of these VEPs except (e). It remains plausible that his belief failed to constitute knowledge. Furthermore, it remains plausible that his belief failed to possess another highly significant VEP—being capable of giving rise to fact-grounded actions. While Harry's belief, in possessing (e), enabled him to purchase a used car because he wasn't going to win, Tom's belief, in lacking (e), failed to enable him to do likewise.[44]

7 Conclusive Reasons and Knowledge

We will now engage in a detailed investigation of ConclusiveReasonsAK. The key feature of this analysis is that beliefs constitute knowledge only if they are based on reasons that wouldn't obtain if the beliefs weren't true. The basing relation "is the relation which holds between a reason and a belief if and only if the reason is a reason for which the belief is held."[45] What exactly is involved in a belief's being based on a reason? Dretske's answer to this question is implicit in the following formulation of his analysis:

S *has conclusive reasons*, R, for believing P if and only if:

(A) R is a conclusive reason for P ...,

(B) S believes, without doubt, reservation, or question, that P is the case and he believes this on the basis of R,

(C) (i) S knows that R is the case or

(ii) R is some experiential state of S (about which it may not make sense to suppose that S *knows* that R is the case; at least it no longer makes much sense to ask *how* he knows).

---

[43]Roughly, being *safe* consists of the belief's being such that it would not easily have been false, and being *produced by the exercise of intellectual virtues* consists of the belief's stemming from the employment of perceptual, reasoning, and other intellectual abilities and powers. Additional VEPs that have been explored by theorists include the metaphorically described VEP *being tethered to the truth* and the rather vague and potentially ambiguous VEP *being non-accidentally true*. Many theorists have employed notions similar to the notion of a VEP; cf., e.g., Chisholm's *positive epistemic status* (Chisholm 1977) and William Alston's *epistemic desiderata* (Alston 2005).

[44]Some theorists whose analyses of knowing have the implausible consequence that Tom knew he wouldn't win have contended that knowledge is acquired in such cases. (See, e.g., Lycan 2006). Such theorists, however, would have to reject KnowledgeEfficacy, which is a highly plausible thesis, or to accept the counterintuitive consequence that Tom bought the used car because he wasn't going to win.

[45]Korcz 2015.

With only minor embellishments, to be mentioned in a moment, I believe that S's having conclusive reasons for believing P is *both* a necessary and a sufficient condition for his knowing that P is the case. The appearance of the word 'know' in this characterization (in (Ci)) does not render it circular as a characterization of knowledge since it can be eliminated by recursive application of the three conditions until (Cii) is reached.[46]

Drawing inspiration from this formulation, we proffer the following characterization of the basing relation:

EpistemicBasing: S believes that p on the basis of a reason, R, iff: either (i) R is the reason, or one of the reasons, for which S believes that p, and R consists of one or more experiential states of S; or (ii) S's believing R to be the case is the reason, or one of the reasons, for which S believes that p, and S knows that R is the case.[47]

As the term 'because' is used herein, 'S believes that p because R is the case' is equivalent to 'R is the reason, or one of the reasons, for which S believes that p'. Accordingly, EpistemicBasing can be expressed in the following way:

EpistemicBasing: S believes that p on the basis of a reason, R, iff: either (i) S believes that p because R is the case, and R consists of one or more experiential states of S; or (ii) S believes that p because S believes that R is the case, and S knows that R is the case.

We employ the expression 'experiential state of S' as an abbreviation of 'indicatory experiential state of S', where an *indicatory* experiential state is one that has the functions of indicating that something is the case and of inducing belief that it is the case. Prime examples of indicatory experiential states are: *its appearing to S that p* and *its seeming to S that p*; examples of non-indicatory experiential states are: *S's fearing that p* and *S's longing for it to be the case that p*.

Formulating EpistemicBasing as a stand-alone thesis makes it clear that its acceptability is independent of the acceptability of ConclusiveReasonsAK. Indeed, EpistemicBasing could be accepted by almost any theorist

---

[46]Dretske 1971, pp. 12-13. The "minor embellishments" referred to in this passage are not relevant to present concerns.

[47]EpistemicBasing is an abbreviation of: S believes that p on the basis of a reason, R, if and only if: either (i) R is the reason, or one of the reasons, for which S believes that p, and R consists of at least one indicatory experiential state of S, or (ii) S's believing that R is the case is the reason, or one of the reasons, for which S believes that p, and S knows that R is the case, or (iii) R consists of a combination of reasons that satisfy the conditions specified by (i) and (ii).

whose account of knowledge makes use of the notion of a subject's believing something on the basis of a reason.[48] Clause (i) of EpistemicBasing accommodates the highly plausible, widely accepted view that perceptual and sensory experiences can function as reasons upon which beliefs can be based. Clause (ii), which is highly plausible in its own right, is closely associated with KnowledgeEfficacy. The following thesis is a special case of KnowledgeEfficacy in which S's "action" consists of believing a proposition:

> **KnowledgeEfficacy***: If S believes that q is the case because S believes that p is the case, then if S knows that p is the case, S believes that q is the case because p is the case; in other words, if at least one of S's reasons for believing that q is the case is that S believes that p is the case, then if S knows that p is the case, at least one of S's reasons for believing that q is the case is that p is the case.

Clause (ii) of EpistemicBasing follows from this thesis. Thus, any theorist who accepts KnowledgeEfficacy must accept this clause. Conversely, any theorist who rejects this clause must reject KnowledgeEfficacy.

The following case illustrates ConclusiveReasonsAK and EpistemicBasing. During a guided tour of London Zoo accompanied by his mother, Helen, Jackie saw a zebra-looking animal, X, and believed that it was a zebra on the basis of its appearing to him that X was a zebra, that is, his having this visual experience was among his reasons for believing X to be a zebra. He wouldn't have had this experience if it hadn't been the case that X was a zebra. Clause (i) of EpistemicBasing has the plausible consequence that he believed X to be a zebra *on the basis* of its appearing to him to be one. And ConclusiveReasonsAK has the plausible consequence that his belief qualified as knowledge, for it was true and was based on conclusive reasons.

This situation can be usefully described in terms of *relevant vs. irrelevant alternatives*. Circumstances were such that if it had been the case that what Jackie saw, X, wasn't a zebra, it might have been the case that X was a giraffe, a wildebeest, etc. These possibilities, which can be called *relevant* alternatives to X's being a zebra, were ruled out by his visual experiences, for such animals wouldn't have looked like zebras to him. Granted, what he saw *could* in principle have been a zebra-lookalike, say, a zonkey that closely resembled a zebra, or a mule that was cleverly disguised to look like a zebra.[49] Had Jackie's reasons been sufficient to rule out such an alternative, his knowledge

---

[48]For discussions of reasons upon which beliefs are based, see, e.g., Barker and Adams 2012, Klein 2012, and Korcz 2016.

[49]For a discussion of a zoo visitor's seeing a mule cleverly disguised to look like a zebra, see Dretske 1971.

might have qualified as *certain* knowledge, an extremely valuable (but diffi-cult to obtain) *species* of knowledge that Cartesians and radical skeptics tend to fixate upon. ConclusiveReasonsAK, however, is aimed at specifying nec-essary and sufficient conditions for *knowledge itself*, or *generic knowledge*. Generic knowledge is far more prevalent, though understandably less prized, than its any of its numerous species, some of which will be discussed in detail later. Since there was no zebra-lookalike anywhere in Jackie's vicinity, the possibility of X's being such a lookalike constituted an *irrelevant* alternative that his visual experience did not need to rule out—this possibility *would not* have been actualized if what he saw hadn't been a zebra.

While visiting the Taigan zoo in Crimea, Jackie and Helen saw a zebra-looking animal, Y, and believed that it was a zebra on the basis of its appear-ing to them that Y was a zebra. Jackie's having this experience, however, wasn't a conclusive reason for his belief. Although Y was a zebra, there was a zonkey in the immediate vicinity that looked like a zebra, and if what he saw hadn't been the zebra, it might have been the zonkey and he might have been fooled.[50] Since his belief that Y was a zebra wasn't based on a conclu-sive reason, ConclusiveReasonsAK does not have the implausible conse-quence that the belief constituted knowledge. Helen, a zoologist who was quite familiar with the visible differences between zebras and zonkeys, be-lieved that Y was a zebra on the basis of its appearing to her that this was the case. If what she saw hadn't been a zebra, it might have been the zonkey, but it wouldn't have appeared to her to be a zebra—in virtue of her expertise, she wouldn't have been fooled. Since Helen believed that Y was a zebra on a basis of a conclusive reason, ConclusiveReasonsAK has the plausible conse-quence that her belief qualified as knowledge.

8   Varieties of Knowledge

In the cases involving Helen and Jackie, Helen alone was in a position to acquire what can be called *contrastive knowledge*. Suppose that in each case she believed that the animal she saw was a zebra *rather than* a zonkey. (To highlight the distinction between saying that something is A *rather than* B, on the one hand, and merely saying that something is A *and not* B, on the other, we will always italicize 'rather than'.) Since Helen was a zoologist who was very familiar with the visible differences between zebras and zonkeys, X's appearing to her to be a zebra constituted not only a conclusive reason for her believing that it was a zebra, but also a conclusive reason for her believing that it wasn't a zonkey. Consequently, her belief qualified not only as *generic knowledge* that X was a zebra and not a zonkey, but also as

---

[50]A zonkey was recently on display in the Taigan zoo. (Guardian Online, August 7th, 2014)

contrastive knowledge that X was a zebra *rather than* a zonkey. Her visual experience functioned as a *differentiator* that enabled her to distinguish between the two possibilities, X's being a zebra and X's being a zonkey. Contrastive knowledge, which is a highly valuable species of knowledge, can be explicated as follows:

> **ContrastiveKnowledge**: S knows that x is A *rather than* B iff x's being A entails x's not being B, and S believes that x is A and not B on the basis of a *contrastively conclusive reason*, R, i.e., (i) if it weren't the case that x is A, then R wouldn't be the case, (ii) if it were the case that x is B, then R wouldn't be the case, and (iii) R doesn't entail either x's being A or x's not being B.[51]

As we'll discuss later, Jackie was capable of acquiring knowledge that X wasn't a zonkey via inference from the fact that X was a zebra and the fact that being a zebra implies not being a zonkey. Hence, he could acquire *generic* knowledge that X was a zebra and not a zonkey. Nevertheless, since his visual experience could not function as a suitable differentiator that would enable him to distinguish between the two possibilities, X's being a zebra and X's being a zonkey, he couldn't acquire *contrastive* knowledge that X was a zebra *rather than* a zonkey.

As the following considerations indicate, ConclusiveReasonsAK has plausible consequences regarding cases of testimonial knowledge, memory knowledge, and introspective knowledge. Lucy, pointing to a swan, X, tells Ethan that it's a swan, and he believes that it's a swan because he experiences her saying so. Clause (i) of EpistemicBasing implies that he believes that X is a swan on the basis of having this experience. If it weren't the case that X is a swan, then it wouldn't be the case that he has the experience, for Lucy knows it's a swan and wouldn't say that it is if it weren't so. Hence, his belief is based on a conclusive reason, and ConclusiveReasonsAK has the plausible consequence that it qualifies as knowledge.

Maria, pointing to a goose, X, tells Ethan that it's a goose, and he believes that this is the case because he experiences her saying so. Clause (i) of EpistemicBasing implies that he believes that X is a goose on the basis of having this experience. But she believes that X is a heron, and is trying to deceive him. If it weren't the case that X is a goose, it might be the case that he has the experience, for she might say that X is a goose even if it weren't so.

---

[51]It should be noted that when S possesses *contrastive* knowledge that x is A *rather than* B, x's being B constitutes a *relevant alternative* to x's being A even if x's being B is a remote possibility that S's reasons wouldn't need to rule out in order for S to possess generic knowledge that x is A. See Barker and Adams 2010 for a more precise explication of contrastive knowledge and for discussion of the function of Clause (iii).

Hence, his belief is not based on a conclusive reason, and ConclusiveReasonsAK does not have the implausible consequence that it qualifies as knowledge.

Sven believes that he saw an eagle last year because he seems to remember that he did, that is, he has the experience of "seemingly remembering" that he did. Clause (i) of EpistemicBasing implies that he believes that he saw an eagle last year on the basis of having this memory experience. If it weren't the case that he saw an eagle last year, then it wouldn't be the case that he has the experience. Hence, his belief is based on a conclusive reason, and ConclusiveReasonsAK has the plausible consequence that it qualifies as knowledge.

Mia believes that the eye chart looks blurry to her, and her reason for believing this is that she experiences the chart's looking blurry. Clause (i) of EpistemicBasing implies that her belief is based on this experience. If it weren't the case that the chart looks blurry to her, then it wouldn't be the case that she has the experience. Hence, her belief is based on a conclusive reason, and ConclusiveReasonsAK has the plausible consequence that it qualifies as knowledge.[52]

9   Knowledge-Closure

The plausible thesis:

> **InferentialReasons**: If S infers that q from the premises that p_1 and that p_2, then S believes that q because S believes that p_1 and p_2, i.e., S's believing that p_1 and p_2 constitutes at least one of S's reasons for believing that q.

together with ConclusiveReasonsAK and EpistemicBasing, imply the knowledge-closure thesis mentioned earlier in the paper:

> **KnowledgeClosure**: If S knows that p and that p implies q, then if S correctly infers that q from the premises that p and p implies q, S knows that q.

Knowing that X was a zebra and that being a zebra implies being a mammal, Jackie inferred that X was a mammal. It follows from InferentialReasons that he believed that X was a mammal because he believed that it was a zebra and

---

[52]In cases of introspective knowledge of experiential states, S's beliefs about her own experiential states are typically based *immediately* upon her being in such states—S's reason for believing that she is in the state consists of her being in the state, and there is no additional reason of hers that mediates this process. (There are, no doubt, *causal factors* that mediate the process.)

being a zebra implies its being a mammal. Given that he knew these premises to be true, Clause (ii) of EpistemicBasing has the consequence that Jackie believed that X was a mammal on the basis of reasons consisting of its being the case that X was a zebra and being a zebra implies being a mammal. It wouldn't have been the case that this reason obtained if it hadn't been the case that X was a mammal; in other words, this reason constituted a conclusive reason for the conclusion belief. ConclusiveReasonsAK has the plausible consequence that the conclusion belief that X was a mammal qualified as generic knowledge, for it was true and was based on a conclusive reason.[53]

Thus, ConclusiveReasonsAK is not only compatible with Knowledge-Closure, but implies it. This constitutes a highly significant development, as it nullifies one of the most damaging criticisms of the Dretskean view and thereby removes a major obstacle that has impeded wider acceptance of the view. Furthermore, the fact that ConclusiveReasonsAK implies knowledge-closure appears to undermine influential arguments for some of its competitors.[54] But how are we to account for the fact that Dretske himself would be apt to reject KnowledgeClosure—after all, he argued against similar knowledge-closure theses.[55] We think that the principal intuitions that seem to militate against acceptance of KnowledgeClosure can be accounted for by attending to the distinction between generic knowledge and contrastive knowledge.

Consider the following modified version of the case involving Jackie at London Zoo. Jackie saw a zebra, X, and believed that it was a zebra because it appeared to him to be one. He wouldn't have had this experience if it hadn't been the case that X was a zebra. Clause (i) of EpistemicBasing has the consequence that Jackie believed X to be a zebra on the basis of its appearing to him to be one; and ConclusiveReasonsAK has the consequence that his belief qualified as generic knowledge. At this point Jackie heard someone in the tour group raise the question of whether X might be a zonkey. Although he didn't know what zonkeys looked like, he knew that they were zebra-donkey hybrids, and therefore weren't zebras. He drew the conclusion that X wasn't a zonkey, and thereby acquired generic knowledge that X wasn't a zonkey. Since he liked zebras and didn't like zonkeys, he photographed X because he believed that it was a zebra and not a zonkey. KnowledgeEfficacy has the

---

[53]In some cases inferential knowledge can be acquired even if the premises aren't known and aren't even true. See Adams, Barker and Clarke 2018 for discussion of the capacity of a Dretskean analysis of knowing to account for such cases.

[54]For example, safety accounts and reliable process accounts have been claimed to be superior to conclusive reasons accounts on the grounds that they are compatible with knowledge-closure (see, e.g., Luper 2016 for discussion).

[55]See, e.g., Dretske 1971 and 2005. (On a personal note, we attempted to persuade Dretske that his own analysis of knowing validated KnowledgeClosure, but we were unsuccessful.)

plausible consequence that he photographed X because it was a zebra and not a zonkey.

Jackie then heard Mildred repeat her statement that X was a zonkey, and, as a result, he was no longer justified in believing that X was a zebra and not a zonkey. Nevertheless, his belief still qualified as *generic* knowledge. Stubbornly refusing to accept Mildred's statement as true, Jackie inferred that X was a zebra *rather than* a zonkey, and he photographed X because he believed that X was a zebra *rather than* a zonkey. But his visual experience, unlike Helen's, was incapable of functioning as a *differentiator* that could enable him to distinguish between the two possibilities, X's being a zebra and X's being a zonkey. Consequently, his inference failed to provide him with *contrastive* knowledge. As we remarked above, KnowledgeClosure had the plausible consequence that Jackie acquired *generic* knowledge that X was a zebra and not a zonkey; but it doesn't have the implausible consequence that in this case he acquired *contrastive* knowledge that X was a zebra *rather than* a zonkey.[56] Furthermore, KnowledgeEfficacy doesn't have the implausible consequence that in this case he photographed X because it was a zebra *rather than* a zonkey.

10 Justification-Closure and Radical Skepticism

The traditional Justified-True-Belief analysis of knowing has been shown to be subject to numerous counterexamples. Many of these counterexamples are closely associated with plausible *justification-closure* theses like the following one:

> **JustificationClosure:** If S is justified in believing that p and that p implies q, then if S correctly infers that q from the premises that p and p implies q, S is justified in believing that q.

Gettier, a pioneer in developing counterexamples to the traditional analysis that invoke a justification-closure thesis, devised an influential argument that

---

[56]See Barker and Adams 2010 for discussion of the following closure thesis for contrastive knowledge:

> **ContrastiveKnowledgeClosure:** If (i) S knows that x is A; (ii) S knows that x's being A entails x's not being B; (iii) S infers that x is A *rather than* B; and (iv) S believes x is A on the basis of a contrastively conclusive reason for believing that x is A and not B; then S has contrastive knowledge that x is A *rather than* B.

Unlike Jackie's visual experience, Helen's could function as a differentiator that enabled her to distinguish between the two possibilities, X's being a zebra and X's being a zonkey. Hence, as this closure thesis implies, she could have acquired knowledge that X was a zebra *rather than* a zonkey.

can be succinctly expressed as follows. He began with two plausible premises:

> First, in that sense of 'justified' in which S's being justified in believing P is a necessary condition of S's knowing that P, it is possible for a person to be justified in believing a proposition that is in fact false. Secondly, for any proposition P, if S is justified in believing P, and P entails Q, and S deduces Q from P and accepts Q as a result of this deduction, then S is justified in believing Q.[57]

Suppose Smith justifiedly believes that Jones owns a Ford on the basis of strong evidence (say, Smith remembers that Jones has always owned a Ford in the past, Jones just offered Smith a ride in a Ford, etc.), even though Jones doesn't own a Ford at the present time. In virtue of Gettier's first premise, this supposition is unobjectionable. Suppose also that Smith competently deduces that either Jones owns a Ford or Brown is in Barcelona, a conclusion that is true because (unbeknownst to Smith) Brown happens to be in Barcelona. In virtue of Gettier's second premise, it follows that Smith justifiedly believes the true proposition that either Jones owns a Ford or Brown is in Barcelona. It is intuitively clear, however, that Smith does not know that this proposition is true. Thus, the traditional analysis turns out to be unacceptable.

The following considerations show that despite its initial plausibility, Gettier's second premise gives rise to radical skepticism. A skeptic could argue along the following lines: "Assume for the sake of the argument that: (i) Edmund justifiedly believes that the creature in front of him is a duck on the basis of its seeming to him to waddle just like a duck; and (ii) he competently deduces that the creature isn't a duck-doppelganger, i.e., a duck-robot that, owing to massive deception by evil geniuses, seems to him to waddle just like a duck. In virtue of Gettier's second premise, it follows that Edmund justifiedly believes that the creature isn't a duck-doppelganger. But he doesn't justifiedly believe this, since believing it not more reasonable from his perspective than suspending judgment regarding it. The evidence for his premise belief is incapable of justifying his conclusion belief, for if the creature were a duck-doppelganger, he would nonetheless possess precisely the same evidence he now has for its being a duck. Consequently, the two assumptions cannot both be true. And since (ii) is unobjectionable, (i) must be rejected. An analogous argument could easily be devised to discredit any claim that someone possesses a justified belief. But possessing such a belief is a necessary condition for possessing knowledge. Consequently, no one really possesses any knowledge."

It might appear at first glance that the skeptic's argument could be discredited by contending that Edmund's evidence really isn't good enough. But

---

[57]Gettier 1963, p. 121.

the skeptic could easily revise the argument to handle this contention: "Assume for the sake of the argument that: (i) Edmund justifiedly believes that the creature in front of him is a duck on the basis of its seeming to him to waddle just like a duck, and to quack just like a duck, and to look just like a duck, ...; and (ii) he competently deduces that the creature isn't a duck-doppelganger, i.e., a duck-robot that, owing to massive deception by evil geniuses, seems to him to waddle just like a duck, and to quack just like a duck, and to look just like a duck, ... In virtue of Gettier's second premise, it follows that Edmund justifiedly believes that the creature isn't a duck-doppelganger. But he doesn't justifiedly believe this, since believing it is not more reasonable from his perspective than suspending judgment regarding it. The evidence for his premise belief is incapable of justifying his conclusion belief, for if the creature were a duck-doppelganger, he would nonetheless possess precisely the same evidence he now has for its being a duck. Consequently, the two assumptions cannot both be true. And since (ii) is unobjectionable, (i) must be rejected. An analogous argument could easily be devised to discredit any claim that someone possesses a certain justified belief. But possessing such a belief is a necessary condition for possessing knowledge. Consequently, no one really possesses any knowledge."

Fortunately for Gettier, his second premise could be replaced with a much weaker premise, one that is far more plausible—"Secondly, in at least some cases, if S is justified in believing P, and P entails Q, and S deduces Q from P and accepts Q as a result of this deduction, then S is justified in believing Q." It is intuitively clear that Smith's conclusion that either Jones owns a Ford or Brown is in Barcelona is one of these cases, for it is a true, competently deduced proposition that he justifiedly believes but does not know to be true. Thus Gettier's counterexamples to the traditional analysis of knowing do not depend for their effectiveness upon unacceptable theses like JustificationClosure.

Defenders of justificationist analyses have often faulted conclusive-reasons analyses for invalidating theses like KnowledgeClosure. As we have seen, our conclusive reasons analysis validates KnowledgeClosure. Ironically, however, justificationist analyses appear to be incapable of validating KnowledgeClosure without the help of JustificationClosure, which the above considerations show to be unacceptable.

Conclusion

Many theorists have distinguished between types of knowledge that have relatively weak requirements on the one hand, and types of knowledge that have stronger requirements on the other.[58] Ernest Sosa, for instance, has distinguished between

> ...two sorts of knowledge, the animal and the reflective: 'knowledge' sometimes means the first, sometimes the second. This is not necessarily to say that the word itself is ambiguous in English. Perhaps the distinction is made through contextual or pragmatic devices that draw on the context of discussion. In any case, animal knowledge that p does not require that the knower have an epistemic perspective on his belief that p, a perspective from which he endorses the source of that belief, i.e., from which he can see that source as reliably truth conducive. Reflective knowledge that p does by contrast require such a perspective.[59]

Keith Lehrer has discussed a strong type of knowledge he calls *metaknowledge*:

> I am concerned with fully human knowledge in which one knows that the information one receives is correct and can, in principle, articulate the information that one receives. This concern is, moreover, not an arbitrary one. What is characteristic of human knowledge is that we can, at least in principle, evaluate whether the information we receive or recall is correct. When, moreover, people are unable to evaluate the information that p which they receive or recall—when, for example, they have no idea whether what they have thus seen, heard, or recalled is correct—then we are disposed to conclude that they do not know whether what they have seen, heard, or recalled is true. They do not, in such cases, really know that p. This is, of course, consistent with admitting that in some weaker sense of the word, they do know. Those senses of the word do not, however, capture the sense of knowledge which is characteristically human, which distinguishes us from other beings. Characteristically human knowledge might be called "advanced" knowledge, or, since it involves the higher-level evaluation of information, it might with equal right be called "metaknowledge."[60]

We have argued that ConclusiveReasonsAK specifies necessary and sufficient conditions for knowledge itself, or *generic knowledge*. (The label

---

[58]Some theorists have held that the term 'know' and its cognates have several different senses (see, e.g., Malcolm 1952); and some have held that contextual aspects of knowledge attributions affect the truth conditions of the attributions in ways that can make it appear that 'know' and its cognates have several different senses (for discussion of a variety of such views, see, e.g., Rysiew 2016). Although we think that the distinction between generic knowledge and various species of knowledge can help account for many of the intuitions that support these views, treatment of this matter is beyond the scope of this paper.

[59]From an interview with Ernest Sosa in EPhilosopher, http://www.ernestsosa.com/interviews.html.

[60]Lehrer 1988, pp. 253-254.

'generic knowledge', we think, is more informative and less apt to mislead than Sosa's 'animal knowledge' and Lehrer's 'information'.) In our opinion, massive funds of generic knowledge can be readily acquired not only by cognitively normal individuals, but also by individuals with impairments such as dementia and autism, and even by very young children.[61] Furthermore, such generic knowledge, owing to its relatively undemanding requirements, is often retained in spite of acquiring misleading information that compromises the reasonability of the belief, or encountering conflicting false opinions that are difficult to refute, or forgetting the source of the information, or experiencing diminished confidence over time.

We have discussed how the conditions required for generic knowledge, together with additional conditions describing various VEPs—Value-Enhancing Properties of beliefs—can be taken to specify necessary and sufficient conditions for certain *species of knowledge*. Several species of knowledge involving VEPs that exceed the minimum requirements for generic knowledge are of special significance for epistemology because beliefs that possess them are apt to be confused with knowledge itself:

- **JustifiedKnowledge**: S possesses *justified* knowledge that p iff S knows that p on the basis of reasons that make S justified in believing that p.

Being justified in believing that p is a VEP that facilitates S's making rational decisions pertaining to initiation, continuation, or termination of inquiry regarding p. Since S can normally determine whether or not her belief that p is justified, acquiring *justified knowledge* provides her with true belief that is typically sensitive to the potential need for engaging in inquiry, and is often an outcome of inquiry. Accordingly, justified knowledge is apt to be less precarious than mere generic knowledge.

- **TenableKnowledge**: S possesses *tenable* knowledge that p iff S knows that p on the basis of reasons that make S indefeasibly justified in believing that p.

Being indefeasibly justified in believing a proposition is a VEP that ensures that S's justification cannot be legitimately defeated by acquisition of additional information. Acquiring *tenable knowledge* provides S with knowledge that is very stable and typically capable of withstanding attempted refutations.

---

[61]The question of whether generic knowledge can be acquired by infants, animals, computer-guided robots, etc. is a complex one that lies beyond the scope of this paper.

- **CertainKnowledge**: S possesses *certain* knowledge that p iff S knows that p on the basis of reasons that provide S with justified certitude that p.

Being based on reasons that afford justified certitude is a VEP that can warrant performing risky actions in situations involving high stakes. Acquiring *certain knowledge*, which Cartesians and radical skeptics have tended to focus exclusively upon, is far more valuable than acquiring "mere" generic knowledge, "mere" justified knowledge, and "mere" tenable knowledge.

- **CriticalKnowledge**: S possesses *critical* knowledge that p iff S knows that p on the basis of *critical reasons*, i.e., reasons that are such that S wouldn't believe that p if these reasons failed to provide S with knowledge that p.

Being based on critical reasons is a VEP that is strongly associated with having trustworthy beliefs—if S possesses critical knowledge that p, then S's opinion regarding p can be trusted not only to be true and well-founded, but also to qualify as knowledge.[62] Acquiring critical knowledge typically requires critical thinking and "healthy skepticism" in order to avoid acquiring beliefs that fail to qualify as knowledge.

- **ContrastiveKnowledge**: S possesses *contrastive* knowledge that it's the case that p *rather than* the case that q iff S knows that it's the case that p and the case that not-q on the basis of conclusive reasons that can differentiate between its being the case that p and its being the case that q.

Being based on reasons that can differentiate between important alternatives is a VEP that is invaluable in situations in which ordinary knowledge fails to rule out such alternatives. Acquiring *contrastive knowledge* typically requires expertise, training, and experience that exceed what is needed for acquiring knowledge itself.[63]

Some VEPs, such as being safe and being produced by reliable, truth-conducive processes, are entailed by the VEP that, we have argued, turns true belief into generic knowledge, viz. being based on conclusive reasons. Some

---

[62]An individual who possesses critical knowledge, however, is not necessarily a *trustworthy informant*, for the individual's belief may be undetectable owing to deception, inability to communicate accurately, etc.

[63] For discussions of these and several other species of knowledge, see Barker 1972, Adams, Barker, and Clarke 2016, 2017, and 2018; and Barker and Adams 2010 and 2012.

other VEPs, such as being based on reasons that make for justified knowledge, for certain knowledge, for critical knowledge, and for contrastive knowledge, add significant value to generic knowledge. The history of epistemology provides good evidence that it is quite difficult to determine precisely which VEP or combination of VEPs enable true beliefs to constitute knowledge itself. Being based on conclusive reasons is a VEP that not only seems to accomplish this, but also seems to account for the ability to engage in fact-grounded actions, that is, the ability to do things for reasons that are facts. There is good evidence, we conclude, that this VEP is the key to the understanding of knowledge that epistemologists have been seeking.[64]

Personal notes by the authors on Fred Dretske

An anecdote from Fred Adams:

I met Fred Dretske in 1974 when I arrived at the University of Wisconsin as first year Ph.D. student. It was at a summer picnic. Dretske was going on sabbatical leave, so I would not see him again for a year. He was working on *Knowledge and the Flow of Information*. I got to know him better in 1975 fall when I took his seminar on the book manuscript, but I am sure I did not impress him. It wasn't until I took an independent study with him the next semester (Spring 1976) on the manuscript that I think he saw something in me. I did get him to make changes in the book and he thanked me for it in the credits (he took out some "contextualist" leanings that I convinced him were contrary to his information-based account of knowledge).

Later, in 1978, I got a Fulbright Fellowship to go to the University of Bristol to study with Andrew Woodfield, Dan Dennett, and Steve Stich. It was very exciting and Dretske and I corresponded the whole time (the old fashioned way—via snail mail). When I returned to Wisconsin I was in Elliott Sober's office. Elliot arrived at Wisconsin the same year I did (only he was Assistant Professor). Elliott became my advisor and had been since 1974. Elliott asked me "so, who will direct your dissertation?" I said "You, since you've been my advisor from the start." About that time Dretske walked in and asked "what are you talking about?" I said we were talking about who should direct my dissertation. Without hesitation Dretske said "I should!" I looked at Elliott and he at me. No words were spoken, but that is how Dretske became my thesis director. Later it occurred to me that Elliott was an untenured assistant professor at the time and Fred was a senior Full professor much better known in the profession at the time. So it made perfect

---

[64] We have benefited greatly from discussions with Peter Baumann, Murray Clarke, Fred Dretske, Alvin Goldman, Robert Gordon, John Hyman, Ralph Kennedy, Peter Klein, William Lycan, Thomas Paxson, Duncan Pritchard, Ernest Sosa, and John Williams.

sense that, for my future career and the job market, he was the better choice. Elliott, Denny Stampe, and Berent Enç, were all on my committee (and Art Glenberg the outside reader from Psychology). My relationship with Dretske grew over the years and we communicated (via e-mail, when it became available) almost weekly. He helped me at many stages of my career, but this may have been the most important first step.

Here is my favorite joke about Fred. As we were driving across the state line one day into Ohio, a sign said "Entering the Buckeye State." Berent Enç asked, "Fred, what's a Buckeye?" Without hesitation, Fred said, "a small animal that lives deep in the woods and is hardly ever seen." I wasn't sure if Fred didn't know or if he was pulling a joke on Berent who *really* didn't know. I laughed so hard I fell off the back seat onto the floor. They both looked back to see what was wrong with me. It turns out that despite attending Purdue and Minnesota and teaching at Wisconsin, Fred didn't know what a Buckeye was (a large acorn). I told this story to Fred several times in his life and he took it well, with good humor each time.

John Barker comments on Dretske's influence on his philosophical development:

Fred Dretske's views about knowledge had a profound impact on my own thinking before I had the pleasure of meeting him. Although in graduate school I was strongly attracted to the traditional reasons-oriented epistemology of C. I. Lewis and Bertrand Russell, in the late 1960's I abandoned this approach in favor of a naturalistic strategy similar to that of Alvin Goldman and David Armstrong. I devised a fact-sensitive-belief analysis of knowing designed to deal with the problems involving accidentally true beliefs that were highlighted in Edmund Gettier's famous essay. Subsequently, influenced by the justificationist views of Roderick Chisholm, Keith Lehrer and Thomas Paxson, I developed an indefeasibly-justified-true-belief analysis of knowing that was intended to handle such problems from a traditional reasons-oriented viewpoint. Finally, upon realizing that Dretske's conclusive-reasons analysis of knowing solved the accidentally true belief problems by specifying in effect that knowledge involves *fact-sensitive reasons* for belief instead of *fact-sensitive belief*, I collaborated with Fred Adams in developing a Dretske-style analysis that avoided such unpalatable consequences as Dretske's rejection of deductive closure of knowledge. After Adams introduced me to Dretske, I benefited greatly from numerous illuminating conversations with him on many epistemological topics. While we failed to convince him that his conclusive-reasons analysis of knowing was compatible with deductive closure of knowledge, this failure has enabled me to retain healthy worries that he may have been right about this highly controversial issue!

References

Adams, F. 1986. The Function of Epistemic Justification. *Canadian Journal of Philosophy* 16:465-492.

Adams, F. 2004. Knowledge. In Luciano Floridi (ed.), *The Blackwell Guide to the Philosophy of Information and Computing*, ed. L. Floridi, 228-236. Oxford: Basil Blackwell.

Adams, F. 2011. Information & Knowledge, a la Floridi. *Putting Information First: Luciano Floridi and the Philosophy of Information*, ed. Patrick Allo, 84-96. Oxford: Wiley-Blackwell; (originally published in *Metaphilosophy* 41(3):331-344).

Adams, F. 2014. Revised Tracking: Cure is Worse than Disease. *Teorema* XXXIII/3:149-158.

Adams, F. and Clarke, M. 2005. Resurrecting the Tracking Theories. *Australasian Journal of Philosophy* 83:207-221.

Adams, F. 2016a. Two Non-Counterexamples to Tracking Theories of Knowledge. *Logos & Episteme* 7:67-73.

Adams, F. 2016b. Rejoinder to Haze. *Logos & Episteme* 7:227-230.

Adams, F., Barker, J., and Figurelli, J. 2012. Towards Closure on Closure. *Synthese* 188:179-196.

Adams, F., Barker, J., and Clarke, M. 2016. Beat the (Backward) Clock. *Logos & Episteme* 7:353-361.

Adams, F. 2018 (forthcoming): Knowledge as Fact-Tracking True Belief. *Manuscrito* (Special issue on epistemology).

Alston, W. 2005. *Beyond Justification: Dimensions of Epistemic Evaluation*. Ithaca, N.Y.: Cornell University Press.

Alvarez, M. 2016. Reasons for Action: Justification, Motivation, Explanation. *The Stanford Encyclopedia of Philosophy*, ed. Edward N. Zalta. URL = <https://plato.stanford.edu/archives/win2016/entries/reasons-just-vs-expl/>.

Anderson, A. and Belnap, N. 1975. *Entailment: The Logic of Relevance and Necessity, Vol. I*. Princeton: Princeton University Press.

Anderson, A., Belnap, N. and Dunn, J. 1992. *Entailment: The Logic of Relevance and Necessity, Vol. II*. Princeton: Princeton University Press.

Ayer, A. J. 1956. *The Problem of Knowledge*. London: Harmondsworth Publishing Company.

Bacon, J. 1971. The Subjunctive Conditional as Relevant Implication. *Philosophia* 1:61-80.

Barker, J. 1969. *A Formal Analysis of Conditionals*. Carbondale, Ill: Southern Illinois University Monographs.

Barker, J. 1972. Knowledge and Causation. *Southern Journal of Philosophy* 9:313-324.

Barker, J. 1976. What You Don't Know Won't Hurt You? *American Philosophical Quarterly* 13:303-308.

Barker, J. 2002. Computer Modeling and the Fate of Folk Psychology. *Cyberphilosophy: The Intersection of Philosophy and Computing*, eds. J. Moore and T. Bynum, 26-44. Oxford: Blackwell; (originally published in *Metaphilosophy* 33:31-48).

Barker, J. and Adams, F. 2010. Epistemic Closure and Skepticism. *Logos & Episteme* I(2):221-246.

Barker, J. 2012. Conclusive Reasons, Knowledge, and Action. *Philosophical Issues* 22:35-52.

Baron-Cohen, S. 1995. *Mindblindness: An Essay on Autism and Theory of Mind*. Cambridge, MA: MIT Press.

Belnap, N. 1967. Intensional Models for First Degree Formulas. *Journal of Symbolic Logic* 32:1-22.

BonJour, L. 1980. Externalist Theories of Knowledge. *Midwest Studies in Philosophy* 5:53–73.

BonJour, L. 1987. Nozick, Externalism, and Skepticism. *The Possibility of Knowledge: Nozick and His Critics,* ed. Steven Luper-Foy, 297-314. Totawa, N.J.: Rowman and Littlefield.

BonJour, L. 1998. *In Defense of Pure Reason: A Rationalist Account of A Priori Justification*. Cambridge: Cambridge University Press.

Chisholm, R. 1957. *Perceiving: A Philosophical Study*, Ithaca, N.Y.: Cornell University Press.

Chisholm, R. 1966. *Theory of Knowledge*, 1st edition. Englewood Cliffs, N. J.: Prentice Hall.

Chisholm, R. 1977. *Theory of Knowledge*, 2nd edition. Englewood Cliffs, N. J.: Prentice Hall.

Clarke, M., Adams, F. and Barker, J. 2017. Methods Matter: Beating the Backward Clock. *Logos & Episteme* 8:99-112.

Dretske, F. 1971. Conclusive Reasons. *Australasian Journal of Philosophy* 49:1-22.

Dretske, F. 2005. Reply to Hawthorne. *Contemporary Debates in Epistemology*, ed. M. Steup and E. Sosa, 43-46. Malden, MA: Blackwell.

Feldman, R. 1994. In Defense of Closure. Presented at the Pacific Division meeting of the American Philosophical Association.

Gettier, E. 1963. Is Justified True Belief Knowledge? *Analysis* 23:121-123.

Goldman, A. 1979. What is Justified Belief? *Justification and Knowledge*, ed. George Pappas, 1-25. Dordrecht: Reidel.

Goldman, A. 1986. *Epistemology and Cognition*. Cambridge, MA: Harvard University Press.

Goldman, A. and Beddor, B. 2016. Reliabilist Epistemology. *The Stanford Encyclopedia of Philosophy*, ed. E. Zalta, URL = <https://plato.stanford.edu/archives/win2016/entries/reliabilism/>.

Goodman, N. 1955. *Fact, Fiction and Forecast*. New York: Bobbs-Merrill.

Gordon, R. and Barker, J. 1994. Autism and the Theory of Mind Debate. *Philosophical Psychopathology* eds. G. Graham and G. Stevens, 163-181. Cambridge, MA: MIT Press.

Hilpinen, R. 1971. Knowledge and Justification. *Ajatus* 33:7-39.

Hyman, J, 2006. Knowledge and Evidence. *Mind* 115:891-916.

Hyman, J. 2010. The Road To Larissa. *Ratio* 23:393–414.

Hyman, J. 2015. *Action, Knowledge, and Will*, Oxford: Oxford University Press.

Klein, P. 1971. A Proposed Definition of Propositional Knowledge. *The Journal of Philosophy* 68:471-482.

Klein, P. 1981. *Certainty: A Refutation of Scepticism*. Minneapolis: University of Minnesota Press.

Klein, P. 2012. What makes knowledge the most highly prized form of true belief? *The Sensitivity Principle in Epistemology*, eds. K. Becker and T. Black, 152-169. New York: Cambridge University Press.

Ichikawa, J. and Steup, M. 2017. The Analysis of Knowledge. *The Stanford Encyclopedia of Philosophy*, ed. E. Zalta, forthcoming URL = <https://plato.stanford.edu/archives/fall2017/entries/knowledge-analysis/>.

Korcz, K. 2015. The Epistemic Basing Relation. *The Stanford Encyclopedia of Philosophy*, ed. E. Zalta, URL = <https://plato.stanford.edu/archives/fall2015/entries/basing-epistemic/>.

Lehrer, K. 1988. Metaknowledge: Undefeated Justification. *Synthese* 74:329-347.

Lehrer, K. and Paxson, T. 1969. Knowledge: Undefeated Justified True Belief. *The Journal of Philosophy* 66:225-237.

Luper, S. 2016. Epistemic Closure. *The Stanford Encyclopedia of Philosophy*, ed. E. Zalta, URL = <https://plato.stanford.edu/archives/spr2016/entries/closure-epistemic/>.

Luper-Foy, S. 1987. The Possibility of Skepticism. *The Possibility of Knowledge: Nozick and His Critics*, ed Steven Luper-Foy, 219-241. Totawa, N.J.: Rowman and Littlefield.

Lycan, W. 2006. On the Gettier Problem Problem. *Epistemology Futures,* ed. Stephen Hetherington, 148-168. Oxford: Oxford University Press.

Malcolm, N. 1952. Knowledge and Belief. *Mind* 61:178-189.

Mares, E. 2004. *Relevant Logic: A Philosophical Interpretation*. Cambridge: Cambridge University Press.

McLaughlin, B. 2016. *Goldman and His Critics*, Oxford: John Wiley and Sons.

Plantinga, A. 1993. *Warrant: The Current Debate*. Oxford: Oxford University Press.

Rysiew, P. 2016. Epistemic Contextualism. *The Stanford Encyclopedia of Philosophy*, ed. E. Zalta, URL = <https://plato.stanford.edu/archives/win2016/entries/contextualism-epistemology/>.

Ramsey, F. 1931. General Propositions and Causality. *Foundations of Mathematics and other Logical Essays,* ed. F. Ramsey, 237-257. Oxford: Routledge and Keagan Paul.

Shope, R. 1983. *The Analysis of Knowing: A Decade of Research*, Princeton: Princeton University Press.

Sosa, E. 1999. How to Defeat Opposition to Moore. *Philosophical Perspectives* 13:141-153.

Steup, M. 2017. Epistemology. *The Stanford Encyclopedia of Philosophy*. ed. E. Zalta, forthcoming URL = <https://plato.stanford.edu/archives/fall2017/entries/epistemology/>.

Swain, M. 1974. Epistemic Defeasibility. *American Philosophical Quarterly* 11:15-25.

Travers, E., Frith, C., and Shea, N. 2018. Learning Rapidly about the Relevance of Visual Cues Requires Conscious Awareness. *Quarterly Journal of Experimental Psychology*, 71(8):1698-1713.

3

Representation and Possibility

JOHN PERRY

Introduction

I hear a knock at the door. Who might that be? Perhaps a lawyer with a large check from the estate of a long forgotten aunt? Perhaps the sweat shirt I ordered weeks ago? Perhaps it's Paul Skokowski, stopping to remind me to work on this paper. I open the door. It's Paul. Two possibilities eliminated. Information eliminates possibilities. This is a key idea in Fred Dretske's account of information and representation.

But what kind of possibilities are eliminated? The standard answer nowadays is that they are sets of possible worlds. These "worlds" are really universes, stretching far beyond our planet, solar system and galaxy, and that's just the beginning. There are an infinity of these possible universes. The information I get when I open the door is that the one I inhabit belongs to the set of possible universes where Paul Skokowski is at my door now. An infinity of possibilities, of possible universes I might inhabit, are eliminated. With all due respect to the great philosophers who have provided us with this account, it strikes me as rather bizarre. I think that by considering Dretske's account of Information and Representation we can come up with something more reasonable.

Information and Mind: The Philosophy of Fred Dretske.
Paul Skokowski (ed.).
Copyright © 2020, CSLI Publications.

In this paper I use Dretske's account to distinguish three kinds of possibilities: Dretskean possibilities, God's possibilities, and Human possibilities. I argue, or at any rate suggest, that the concept of a circumstance found in Frege's *Begriffsschrift* (1879) is the key concept for understanding them. But Frege abandoned what I'll call first level circumstances in his theory of sense and reference. A first level circumstance involves objects having properties and standing in relations. The theory of sense and reference was much more influential in twentieth century philosophy than his *Begriffsschrift*, and circumstances fell into disrepute.

When we look at things in the way I suggest, the centrality of *properties* emerges. Properties are basic to Dretskean possibilities and God's possibilities, and we need them to resuscitate circumstances and understand Human possibilities.

1   A Dretskean Theory of Representation

In *Naturalizing the Mind* (1995), Dretske puts his theory of representation like this:

> The fundamental idea is that a system, S, represents a property, F, if and only if S has the function of indicating (providing information about) the F of a certain domain of objects....
> The way S performs its function . . . is by occupying different states s_1, s_2 . . . s_n corresponding to the different determinate values f_1, f_2, . . . f_n of F. (Dretske, 1995, page 2.)

Dretske's favorite examples are instruments, like altimeters and speedometers, and relatively simple forms of intelligent life that harness information to survive, like magnetosomes. The instruments have the function of indicating some property of some object for the use of the humans who use the instruments. Your altimeters may tell you the altitude of the plane you are flying. Your speedometer may tell you the speed of the car you are driving. The northern hemisphere magnetosome's internal magnet detects magnetic north, providing it information concerning its own position, and the direction of the oxygen-depleted water it needs to survive. So representation seems to involve objects as well as properties. Without the objects you couldn't have an account of truth and falsity, or accuracy or inaccuracy, or veridicality, of representations.

Dretske's account of reference is rather rudimentary; his heart was really never in the philosophy of language as far as I could tell, but rather issues of information and epistemology. I argue in "Reference and Dretske's Theory of Representation" (forthcoming 1) that his account of reference, as far as it goes, isn't very satisfactory, but can be the basis of an illuminating account of the connection between reference and representation. I think it is important to distinguish two somewhat different issues:

1. Do we need to make reference to the objects that have, or are in some sense taken to have, the represented properties, in order to make sense of the system in question?

2. Do we need to attribute a capacity for reference to the system in question?

The first need arises when we make a distinction between true and false, (veridical or non-veridical, accurate or inaccurate, etc.) representations. It is the function of a normal speedometer to indicate the speed of the car in which it is installed. The speed of *that* car is the standard for the accuracy or inaccuracy of the speedometer reading. The user of the speedometer needs to realize this, and we need to as well when we do the "semantics" of speedometers, that is explain what has to be the case for a speedometer to be correct. But typical speedometers do not need to represent *which* car is the one the speed of which they are indicating. Everyone who uses the speedometer knows which car the speed of which is being represented.

In contrast, suppose a highway patrolman has a radar gun which detects the speed of all the cars in all the lanes of the section of the highway it is pointed at, at least those that are not obscured by others. This feature wouldn't be of much use unless there were some way of showing which car went with which speed. As well as representing the speed, the gun has to represent the car *of which* it is the speed. If the gun provides only the speeds at which cars are traveling at the time the trigger is pulled, this could be simply different cells on the screen for cars that are successively further from the gun.

On our Dretskean view, representation is a property of systems *harnessing information.*[1] Such harnessing has three aspects: detection, application, and goal.

Some aspect of a system, which we can call the "sensor", detects information. The sensor has a number of states it can be in at a given time. Which state it is in is determined by effects on it from events outside the sensor, which may be events in the world external to the system, or events within other parts of the system. The kind of event that has these effects is related

---

[1] See Israel and Perry, 1990, 1991.

in a law-like, or at least fairly regular way, to the states produced, and hence carries information about those events.

The changes in the sensor are not only effects but causes. They cause changes in the rest of the system, immediately or eventually, depending on the system, and partly determine what the system does.

The function of the detection and application of information is to further some goal. The change caused should promote the attainment of the goal, given the correctness of the information. It is the combination of detection, change, and goal that makes sense of such a system.

Speedometers, meat thermometers, and other such information detecting devices, provide only the sensors, not the whole system. There is typically a human agent, who supplies the action and the goals and harnesses the information. My speedometer detects that the car of which it is a part is going 75 m.p.h; that causes me, the driver of the car, to become aware of the fact that my car is going 75 mph. That knowledge, combined with my belief that the speed limit is 65 mph and my desire not to get a ticket, causes me to lessen the pressure on the accelerator pedal, which causes the car to slow down, which promotes my goal of not getting a ticket. The meat thermometer detects that the roast into which it is stuck has reaches 155 degrees; the cook, whose goal was to serve it medium rare removes it, promoting that goal. These devices have a function only as part of a system involving an agent, paradigmatically a human.

2   Articulation

When we consider primitive organisms (or even cells) the systems can be quite simple, comparatively speaking at least. The northern hemisphere magnetosome's[2] internal magnet detects magnetic north, providing it information concerning its own position, and the direction of the oxygen-depleted water it needs to survive. The magnetosome is caused to swim in that direction, promoting the goal of survival.

When the theorist looks at the magnetosome, and explains things in terms of harnessing information, she needs to identify and keep track of factors that the magnetosome doesn't worry about: the sensing mechanism, the information it detects and the regularities involved in the detection; the connections between the detection and the action, and the goal that the action promotes. The magnetosome needn't worry about any of these things, even if magnetosomes can worry, which seems unlikely. I'll put this by saying that the theorist must *articulate* --- have ideas and words for ---parameters

---

[2] I'm using "magnetosome" as Dretske does, for the creature, rather than for its magnetic sensor, which seems to be more common.

involved in successful harnessing of information that the system doing the harnessing does not need to articulate.

The term "unarticulated constituent" comes from the philosophy of language. Consider three cases:

(i) My wife looks out the window and says, "It's raining". But there is no such thing as simply *raining*, at least not until global warming gets worse. It rains in a place at a time. She explicitly tells me what is happening—rain—and with the present tense when the rain occurs. But she doesn't explicitly tell me where. Of course, I'm sure she means in Palo Alto, where we are. If she is calling from Copperopolis, then it's not so clear. She might be looking at the weather channel there, and calling me to tell me I don't need to worry about cleaning the gutters today. Or she might just be talking about the weather in Copperopolis.

There can be no assessment of either utterance without determining a place relative to which the claim that it is raining is to be evaluated. We need a circumstance to be a fact or not a fact, or a proposition to be true or not true, and this requires a place. When it's obvious, as in the first case, there is no need to articulate this parameter of the rain relation, to put it pompously. When it's not obvious, articulation is a good idea.

(ii) Elwood tells me, "It's noon". There is no such thing as just being noon. A time is only noon relative to a place or, nowadays, a time-zone. If I know that Elwood is in the same place, or even the same time-zone, as I am, I know what proposition he is expressing. If, for all I know, he is calling from Omaha or Paris, confusion may result if he doesn't tell me what place he is talking about.

Sometimes we turn this to our advantage. It's 2 o'clock in Palo Alto and 5 o'clock in New York. I promise my editor I'll email revisions to her by 5:30, and quickly hang up. She doesn't get them before she goes home at 6 Eastern Time, as she had hoped, but just after I sent them at 5:30 Pacific Time. I didn't exactly lie.

But what if Elwood is an eight-year old, who doesn't know about time-zones and the relativity of "o'clock properties," to locations. Eight-year olds don't need to know about that. At least when I was eight we didn't need to. He won't articulate the missing constituent and say, "It's noon in Palo Alto," or "It's noon in Omaha" because he has no idea what he would be saying. And, as long as Elwood converses only with people in his own time-zone—his parents keep him off the internet—he won't have much need to learn about these issues.

(iii) When we reflect on time-zones, an even deeper level of unarticulated constituents emerges. We didn't always have time-zones. In the distant past, people weren't aware of the fact that noon, when the sun was the highest, occurred at different times in different places. Even when this became known to astronomers, most people weren't aware of it. It just didn't matter. The distance you could travel in a day, even on horseback, wasn't enough to make problems. There was no such thing as horse-lag.

Given the distance travelled by railroads, and the fact that much of the travel was east to west and west to east, things became intolerable in the nineteenth century. Clocks had to be reset every station or so, to coordinate with the local time, and people started becoming aware of the relativity of o'clock properties of times to places. Schedules demanded some system. At one point there were one hundred time-zones in America; the four standard zones were not determined until 1883. Britain had its own system, and then took the lead in getting an international consensus for basically the system we have now.

The o'clock properties have always been relative to location. There is no such thing as simply being noon or one o'clock, and never was. But the location parameter of such properties was irrelevant for most of human history. Then problems with it cropped up, particularly with train-schedules, and articulation was needed.

The general principle suggested is something along the line of we don't articulate a thing until we have to, until the failure to do so leads to misunderstanding. Readers familiar with Heidegger may see this as an instance of the phenomenon of "breakdowns", which are crucial to the process by which humans come to more and more articulated conceptions of their environment and themselves[3].

Unarticulation isn't just something that comes up with names and reference. If we start at the simplest level of representation, articulation is a need that comes with more and more sophisticated means of harnessing information, and the general principle is simply an application of a more general principle that lies deep in the phenomenon of representation. I think this is so important that I will give it a name: *incrementality*. I claim it is not only feature of our use of names, or something needed to understand magnetosomes, but a very basic part of the human condition.

3   What Else?

If your partner asks you to set the table, you won't go to the garage and start building a table. You won't even go to the closet and get a tablecloth. You will glance in the dining room; seeing a table and a tablecloth already in place. You will then get the silverware and the plates and the napkins, and do *what else* needs to be done, to bring about that there is a set table, given what is

---

[3] See Heidegger, 1962, p. 105 (GA 2: 74-75).

already there. This is an example of incrementality. The questions on which we focus usually amount to *what else* has be the case, for a need to be satisfied, a desire to be fulfilled, or a statement to be true, circumstances that we are taking as given.

As Paul Skokowski has shown, (Skokowski 1999; Skokowski 2003) Mackie's concept of an INUS condition is helpful in developing Dretske's ideas. An INUS condition is an Insufficient (on its own) but Necessary (or at least Non-redundant) part of a complex Unnecessary but Sufficient condition for something. (Mackie 1974) Mackie's target was causation. If a hot box causes a freight car to lose a wheel as a fully-loaded train goes around a curve at twenty miles an hour, and the train derails, a commission assigned to figure out what happens might well say that the lost wheel *caused* the derailment. They don't need to suppose that the lost wheel was sufficient on its own to derail the train; they may have concluded that if it had not been moving, or not going around a curve, or not fully loaded, it wouldn't have derailed. But those things, together with the lost wheel, were sufficient. That complex of conditions wasn't necessary however; a missing rail or a well-placed bomb would have been sufficient to derail the train. The lost wheel was an INUS condition.

The commission picked on it for practical reasons. The railroad wants to eliminate such accidents in the future. The railroad isn't likely to eliminate curves, keep its trains at rest, or always leave them only partially loaded. But it can take steps to eliminate wheels falling off cars, by greasing their bearings more often. Which INUS condition we call "the cause" is a practical decision.

In any inquiry, the questions we focus on amount to *what else* has be the case, for a need to be satisfied, a desire to be fulfilled, or a statement to be true, given circumstances that we are taking as given. These may be things we have already established, or assumed for the sake of argument. But they also may be basic facts about the way the world works, at least where we live and our ancestors evolved, to which we are attuned, genetically or by individual experience.

For example, I am (fairly well) attuned to the force of gravity near the surface of the earth, in that I act in ways that work given what it is, but wouldn't work at all if it were different. I'm pretty good at getting a cup of coffee to my lips in a reasonable amount of time without splashing it all over myself. If I were in a spaceship, the same movements would make a mess. Astronauts have to keep track of the force of gravity, but I don't. And millions of people all over the world who have never heard of the force of gravity are more adept than I at getting cups of liquid to their lips without making a mess.

To survive, there have to be things the animal can do that provide what else is necessary, given things already in place, to complete conditions sufficient for gaining nutrition, avoiding enemies, and the like. Pecking won't do a hen any good unless there is a kernel of corn or millet at the point at which her beak will intersect with the ground. If there is, and gravity is normal, and so and so on and so on, by pecking she will complete conditions sufficient for getting a bit of nutrition.

So we can say that the job of representational states is to cause actions that are the INUS conditions for some goal of the systems, *given* what, for one reason or another, can be taken as given. What can be taken will usually be different for the organism involved and the person who is trying to understand the organism. The organism needs to act only when conditions are sufficient for success, or at least when they are likely sufficient for success. The theorist needs to understand why these other factors can be taken as given.

To see the philosophical importance of these ruminations, consider self-knowledge. We can say that the hen who is pecking, or even the magnetosome who is swimming, has a rudimentary form of self-knowledge, simply because the information they get is information about themselves. The hen as I imagine her doesn't have to figure out *which* hen needs to do the pecking to ingest the kernel she sees, or *which* hen will gain nutrition if the pecking is successful. That's all built-in.

But consider a more socially aware hen. She notes not only when there are kernels in front of her, but when there are kernels in front of other chickens. If she sees a mild-mannered smallish hen with a kernel in front, she scares the hen away and pecks it herself. If it is a larger hen or a rooster, she doesn't. Such a hen has to have a state that contains information that there is a chicken with a kernel in front of it at a certain distance and in a certain direction. But that representation will have to be articulated, if she is to be in different states depending on the chicken, or type of chicken, involved. She will be representing the same property, the property of having a kernel in front, in two different ways; articulated for other chickens, but not for herself.

Consider the highway patrol radar gun. An improved version is built into the speedometer of the patrol car. As the patrol car goes down the highway, the speedometer indicates the speeds of cars in front of it, in cells across the top of the display. But it displays the speed of the patrol car itself in the same old way, with a pointer at the bottom.

Animals differ in their ability to pass "the mirror test". If you put some coloring on a chimpanzee's head in a way that he doesn't notice, and then put him in front of a mirror, after a bit he will brush the stuff off the top of his head. A natural interpretation is that the chimpanzee figures out that he is getting information about himself in the same way he usually gets information about other chimps. The information motivates a way of grooming that affects the chimp who performs it, rather than one that affects the chimp in front of it. Chickens don't pass the mirror test, but some birds do. Chimps do, but some simians don't. Human children begin to pass the mirror test at about eighteen months.

4 Three Kinds of Possibility

With all of this in mind, I want to distinguish three kinds of possibilities.
For this purpose, I want to borrow a concept that Frege uses in his *Begriffsschrift* (1879) In this work Frege takes the contents of sentences to be *circumstances*. What I'll call a *basic first level* circumstance consists of objects having properties and standing in relations. The content of the sentence "Heidegger was a philosopher" signifies the circumstance that that individual had that property. As Frege would have put it, it is the circumstance Heidegger *falls under* the *concept, x is a philosopher*. Some circumstances are facts. We can give a "disappearance" account of factuality:

> The circumstance that Heidegger is a philosopher is a fact if and only if Heidegger is a philosopher.

I distinguish circumstances from propositions, and being factual from being true. Propositions and truth, as I see it, are concepts for classifying linguistic and mental representations by one of their crucial properties, their truth-conditions. A disappearance account of truth doesn't work. For example,

> Sartre's belief that Heidegger was a philosopher is true iff Heidegger was a philosopher

isn't right, because for Sartre's belief to be true, Sartre and his belief had to exist, but this is not a necessary condition for Heidegger having been a philosopher.

We might say that the proposition that Heidegger was a philosopher is true iff Heidegger was a philosopher. But for most theories of propositions this won't work. Suppose we take a proposition to be a set of possible worlds. So the proposition that Heidegger was a philosopher is the set of worlds in which he was a philosopher. But Heidegger's having been a philosopher is not sufficient for this set of possible worlds to be a true proposition. Someone had to decide that sets containing the actual world are to be used to classify true beliefs and statements. Being true is not a property such sets have in virtue of their set theoretical properties. It's what Kripke and Lewis and other possible worlds theorists decided would work well as a way of representing truth-conditions of statements and beliefs. It is a natural choice; a philosopher who called a set of worlds "true" if the actual world were not a member of the set would be somewhat perverse. However natural the choice is, however, Heidegger's being a philosopher was not sufficient for the set of worlds in which he is a philosopher to be used in the way possible worlds theorist use it, for classifying true statements and beliefs.

Frege also recognized higher level circumstances, and when he moved from his *Begriffsschrift* theory to his theory of sense and reference, he only recognized higher level circumstances. These involve concepts falling under higher level concepts. The statement "Every philosopher owns a book" consists of the properties of being a philosopher and owning a book falling under the relation that everything that instantiates the first instantiates the second. I'll call any complex circumstance that involves a basic first level circumstance a first level circumstance. So, "Every philosopher owns a book and Heidegger was a philosopher" signifies a first level circumstance, but not a basic one.

The three kinds of possibilities I distinguish, then, I'll regard as circumstances, not as propositions or sets of worlds.

First there are what I'll call Dretskean possibilities.

The hen's eyesight detects properties of herself. There is, or is not, a kernel of corn a certain distance and direction from her. There is, or is not, another chicken nearby her, and so forth. Assume the chicken reacts to *types* of individuals, but not particular individuals. Then the realm of possibilities, for chickens, will consist of properties a chicken may or may not have: having a kernel in front, having a rooster nearby, and so forth. Her possibilities just have to do with properties. If she has a language of thought, it would have to express her mental states in sentences, like "Lo, kernel nearby" and "Lo, no kernel." No reference to herself, and no reference to particular kernels, would be required. From the chicken's point of view, we just have important properties, like there being a kernel in front, being instantiated or not.

As chicken theorists, however, we need first level circumstances. We have to have particular hens and particular kernels of corn in our ontology, to explain what is going on. If a chicken has a "Lo kernel in front" thought, the thought is true only if there is a kernel near the chicken that has it. We will see the hen and the kernels as involved in the veridicality conditions of her perceptions, and the success conditions of the pecking they cause. But for the hen they are *unarticulated* constituents—she doesn't need concrete objects in her ontology. At least my simple-minded chickens don't.

The second kind of possibilities I'll call "God's possibilities." I know even less about God than I do about chickens, of course. For one thing, I'm quite sure there are chickens. But, putting my ignorance aside, suppose things go like this. It's Wednesday of Creation Week. On Monday, God has decided on the laws of logic and mathematics, if she needed to do that. Tuesday she decided what properties and relations she wanted to be exemplified in Her universe, and arrived at what we might think of as an infinity of Ramsey sentences, each of which begins with a very long string of existential quantifiers and continues with specifications of all the properties and relations to be instantiated and co-instantiated. That is, more or less, perhaps squinting a little, God's alternative plans are basically higher level circumstances, involving properties being instantiated by lower-level properties, quantifying over the individuals that do the ultimate instantiating.

On Wednesday morning, God settles on one plan for Creation, one complex circumstance she will make factual, based on further considerations, perhaps including benevolence. Now it's Wednesday afternoon, and time to create the World.

Can God simply say, "Let it be!"? Or does She have to expend more effort, and make some further decisions? Does She need to decide *which* objects are going to do the instantiating? She has decided that the properties of being the first human, living in a perfect garden called "Eden", and having more ribs than needed, and being called "Adam" will be co-instantiated. Does she have a further choice, which objects will do the instantiating and be Adam and the Garden of Eden? Where is the domain of objects from which she would make this choice?

Insofar as I have intuitions about such issues, it doesn't seem that she needs to any such thing. If She just says, or sings, or thinks, "Let it be!" the objects will be taken care of, and there will be lonely Adam in the Garden of Eden with his spare rib. In Fregean terms, it seems that we can think of God as establishing a realm of comprehensive Thoughts, higher-order circumstances, and then deciding which one is to denote Truth.

Once she has done that She can think about Adam, and make decisions about him, for example to expel him from the Garden of Eden. I'll leave aside issues of how the situation that led to this fits with omniscience and benevolence. She can think about Adam in what seems to be a different way. She thinks about an existing individual, and not simply whoever is going to have the properties she has chosen for the first human. My son Jim, who knows more about these things than I do, points out that there are at least hints of this transition in Her thinking as we go from Genesis I to Genesis II.

The third category I'll call "Human possibilities". Consider Maude, a fifth grade teacher. A few days before the term starts, she gets a list of the students she will have, with information about their gender, records through the fourth grade, and photos. Maude has a classroom with thirty desks; she has a list of thirty students. She draws up some alternative seating charts— that is, she considers possibilities for assigning the students on her list to the desks in her classroom. She wants to avoid putting troublesome boys behind girls with long braids, because the boys might put the girls' braids in their inkwells (this all happened some time ago). She wants to put the troublesome boys and girls up front, where she can easily keep an eye on them. Given that, the shorter students should be towards the front, the taller ones further back. And so on.

Maude's possibilities are Human possibilities. They correspond to first level circumstances, with some admixture of higher level circumstances. She has a domain of objects—the students and the desks—to work with, and the relation of "sits in". Her various seating charts represent complex circumstances; distributions of the relevant properties and relations to the objects in the domain. She may bring in higher level possibilities to think about additional students, or new desks, and the various uniformities connecting types of students with kinds of trouble they are likely to cause.

I think that is what Human possibilities are like, even for the most divine among us. As Strawson persuasively argued in *Individuals* (1959), the human world is organized around concrete objects, having properties and standing in relations, enduring through time, changing in ways we can anticipate and ways we cannot. Seating charts are ways of representing possible circumstances. We don't need to regard them as necessary for a description of reality needed by God, or logic, or any finished science; they can, perhaps, all get by with Fregean Thoughts, involving only higher level circumstances and facts about instantiation and co-instantiation of the properties and relations involved in Thoughts. But we need them to understand human thinking and the ordinary languages we use.

This is the concept of possibility that is usually relevant to the concept of information and the phenomenon of communication.

When we communicate we are usually interested in what properties various objects have, and what relations they stand in to other objects. The properties include roles that other objects, possibly not included in the original domain, might play relative to objects in the domain, and then further objects that might play roles relative to them. Whom shall I invite to dinner? Not Tom and not Barbara. Maybe Fred and Alfred. Does Fred have a girlfriend? If so I should invite her too. But what if his girlfriend has a child? Then maybe not, children can be a pain at dinner parties. And so on.

5 The Loss of Human possibilities

When Frege went from the *Begriffsschrift* theory to his theory of sense and denotation, he left out first-order circumstances. At the level of sense we only have properties and relations to work with; there are no objects in senses or Thoughts. At the level of denotation, we have individuals, extensions[4] and truth values.

Frege's theory of sense and reference had tremendous influence in analytical philosophy, once his philosophical essays were translated into English during the middle of the last century. Some philosophers like Quine, didn't like the level of sense. So they try to get by with a level of denotation, with just its objects, extensions and truth values.

The New Theory of Reference, that is, the works of Kripke, Donnellan, Kaplan and others, which emerged in the 1960s and 70s, disclosed a need for Human possibilities in semantics, that is to say, first level circumstances. But circumstances as such were not recognized. Instead "singular propositions" were countenanced; I regard them as faux-circumstances. These are propositions with objects as constituents. There are no such things in Frege's realm of Thoughts; as he said to Russell, Mont Blanc, with all of its snowfields, is not a constituent of any Thought. This led to the project of figuring out how to think of such propositions. If propositions are sets of worlds, don't singular propositions require that we have the same individuals in different possible worlds? The proposition that Heidegger is a philosopher ought to be the set of worlds in which Heidegger himself is a philosopher. "Not so fast," David Lewis said; all we need is the counterpart relation between world-bound individuals.

Without denying the great ingenuity that has gone into this project and the insights that have resulted from it, I suggest we ought to understand possibilities in terms of circumstances, and not the other way around.

If, like Quine, we are to eschew Frege's senses, then it seems that we ought to beef up the level of denotation. In Frege's system, we only find properties in the realm of sense. To get from "is a philosopher" to the extension, we pass through what he calls a concept, a word he uses for properties and relations. But in the theory of sense and reference, concepts are individuated by their extensions, at least for the purposes of serious science. So the concept of having or having had a heart and the property of having or having

---

[4] Frege did not think of extensions quite the way they are now thought of. The extension of "*x* is a philosopher" would not be the set of philosophers, but a course of values. This is pretty close to a set of ordered pairs, with every object there is appearing as a first element, and either Truth or Falsity as the second. What we now call the extension, the set of philosophers, consists of those objects paired with Truth in the course of values.

had a kidney (Quine's example updated to take account of advances in medicine) are basically the same.[5] The attempt to retain extensions as the denotations of predicates leads to the possible worlds analysis of properties as functions from worlds to extensions. But it seems to me properties are a much more basic and intelligible part of life, animal or human, than functions from possible worlds to extensions.

I suggest a return to Frege's *Begriffsschrift* picture: properties, objects, and circumstances.

Conclusion

On Dretske's theory, properties are basic to understanding representation. Sensory states carry information because of regularities between properties of the external world and the properties of organs. The information is harnessed, because of regularities between the properties instantiated in movements and other bodily changes and properties of the world effected by those changes.

But Human possibilities involve not only properties being instantiated but objects having properties. To understand objects and their importance in human thinking, we need to understand the role they play in allowing humans to harness information in more and more complicated ways. Dretske has opened the door, we need to go through it. But to do so, we need to grant circumstances and properties first-class status.

Personal note on Fred Dretske

An anecdote from John Perry:

I met Fred Dretske in the late 1970s, at a colloquium at the University of Cincinnati. I was thrilled to meet him, but had little chance to talk to him at the colloquium. But then we sat together on a flight back to Chicago. That was one of the most exciting hours I have spent in philosophy. I asked him what he was working on, and he enthusiastically explained the basic ideas of *Knowledge and the Flow of Information,* which came out a year or so later. That was my introduction to what Jerry Fodor called "Semantics, Wisconsin Style." Some years later Fred and I became colleagues at Stanford, and Fred and I became good friends, along with Judith and Frenchie. But in many years of pleasant memories and exciting conversations, that trip from Cincinnati to Chicago still stands out.

---

[5] We can't say they are identical, because Frege takes identity to be a relation that hold between objects, and concepts are "unsaturated" and therefore not objects. For more on these topics see Perry, forthcoming 2.

References

Dretske, F. 1995. *Naturalizing the Mind*. Cambridge, MA: MIT Press.

Frege, G. 1879. *Begriffsschrift, eine der arithmetischen nachgebildete Formelsprache des reinen Denkens*. Halle.

Frege, G. 1892. Über Sinn und Bedeutung. *Zeitschrift für Philosophische Kritik* NF 100:25-30.

Heidegger, M. 1962. *Being and Time*. Translated by John Macquarrie & Edward Robinson. Oxford: Blackwells.

Israel, D. and Perry, J. 1990. What is Information? *Information, Language and Cognition*, ed. P. Hanson. Vancouver: University of British Columbia Press.

Israel, D. and Perry, J. 1991. Information and Architecture. *Situation Theory and Its Applications*, Vol. 2, eds. J. Barwise, J. M. Gawron, G. Plotkin, and S. Tutiya. Stanford University: Center for the Study of Language and Information.

Perry, John, forthcoming 1. Reference and Dretske's Theory of Representation. *Themes from Dretske*, ed. Michael Freauchiger. Berlin: de Gruyter.

Perry, John, forthcoming 2. *Frege's Detour*.

Skokowski, P. 1999. Information, Belief and Causal Role. *Logic, Language and Computation*, eds. L. Moss, J. Ginzburg, and M. de Rijke, 318-335. Stanford: CSLI Press.

Skokowski, Paul, 2004. Structural Content. *Philosophy of Science*, (71) 362-379.

Strawson, P.F. 1959. *Individuals*. Abingdon: Routledge.

4

Three Dogmas of Internalism

PAUL SKOKOWSKI

Introduction

A rather common assumption in philosophy of mind, in particular with respect to conscious experience, has been that three famous arguments pose
threats—potentially fatal—to materialism about mind. These are Nagel's
'what it is like' argument, Kripke's 'modal' argument, and Jackson's
'knowledge' argument. This assumption has also led to what is really a kind
of dogma, which is that each of the three arguments apply to all forms of
materialism. Fred Dretske recognized this dogma as well—though in a different context—which he referred to as 'The Internalist Intuition.' (Dretske
1995) However, I think the threats have been misinterpreted. These arguments are not threats to all forms of materialism about mind, but only to internalist theories of mind—those theories that place mental states entirely
within the head of the individual who has them. However, it turns out that
another form of materialism—externalism—evades the arguments entirely.
In this essay I will show problems with these three internalist arguments, and
show how externalist accounts, inspired in part by Dretskean approaches to
the mind, evade Nagel's, Kripke's and Jackson's challenges, and thus dispel
the three dogmas of internalism.

Information and Mind: The Philosophy of Fred Dretske.
Paul Skokowski (ed.).
Copyright © 2020, CSLI Publications.

1   The First Dogma: Nagel's what-it-is-like arguments

Nagel's paper 'What is it like to be a bat?' is critical at a variety of levels of materialism's prospects for explaining conscious experience. However, as is mentioned at several points in the paper, it is not completely dismissive of materialism's potential for explaining conscious experience at some point in the future. To give one example, Nagel states that "It would be a mistake to conclude that physicalism must be false." (Nagel 1974, p. 223) Rather than outright rejection of materialism, Nagel offers instead that it "… is a position we cannot understand because we do not at present have any conception of how it might be true." (Nagel p. 223) Nagel's approach therefore differs from approaches we will soon see from Kripke and Jackson, which do argue for an outright rejection of materialism about mind. Be this as it may, the main thrusts of Nagel's arguments challenging materialism are aimed at internalist conceptions of mind. Non-internalist accounts, like functionalism, Nagel dismisses out of hand as 'neobehaviorist'. He lumps them with more traditional behaviorist accounts, which are themselves, by construction, devoid of any explanation, or even mention, of the subjective nature of experience. (Nagel p. 223) In order to emphasize these neobehaviorist aspects, Nagel says of functionalist accounts "It is useless to base the defense of materialism on any analysis of mental phenomena that fails to deal explicitly with their subjective character." (Nagel, p. 219) So, in Nagel's view, any functionalist account fails, by omission, to even address consciousness and so cannot be taken seriously to give a material, physical account of consciousness. What is left to be considered, then, are internalist accounts.

Nagel addresses with more seriousness the possibility that mental states might be internal bodily/brain states. He does this by considering internalist-style examples, such as an alien species studying an active human brain, and thus perchance, human mental states: "… a Martian investigating my brain might be observing physical processes which were my mental processes…." (Nagel p. 222) And later, Nagel categorizes materialist accounts of mind as being entirely contained within the body: "…the meaning of physicalism is clear enough: mental states are states of the body." (Nagel, p. 222) Nagel is not therefore dismissing internalist mind-brain materialism out of hand, as he has with functionalism: it is at least worth considering that mental states are internal states of an agent. Indeed, when he does take materialism seriously, he unambiguously states that the 'what-it-is-like' aspect of mental states is an intrinsic property of these internal physical states: "If mental processes are indeed physical processes, then there is something it is like, *intrinsically*, to undergo certain physical processes." (Nagel, p. 223, my emphasis) Therefore, internalist conceptions of mind seem to be where the interesting action is for Nagel.

But there is another issue with Nagel's approach which is problematic, and that is: what exactly *is* this notion of what-it-is-like? What-it-is-like appears to include many things. In fact, Nagel appears to be using the term to refer to three distinct notions. The first notion is the following. Consider that if we are talking about a particular mental event token, then what it is like to experience that mental event must include, somehow, all our other occurrent mental states at that time as well. If we are talking about ourselves at a moment in time, then our memories and history will certainly also have an effect on the what-it-is-likeness of our conscious experience at that time. Our conscious mental events do not occur in isolation from the rest of our mental lives, but rather occur within a what I prefer to call our 'mental economy' — an economy that is immediate, vibrant, and ever-changing. Nagel is certainly correct that we can never know what it is like to be a bat, but it's also quite clear that that we cannot know what it is like to be each other. Two humans do not share token beliefs, and they certainly don't share each other's occurrent mental (explicit, implicit, memory, etc) states; our mental economies differ in both their state tokens, and the relations, and more often than not, even the types exemplified by those tokens. Indeed, even identical twins do not share identical mental economies. So, we can never know what it is like to be a bat. And we can never know what it is like to be each other, which is indeed a point that Nagel acknowledges. (Nagel p. 221) But we can't even know what it is was like to be ourselves in childhood. We lack the mental economy *now* that we had back *then*. There are parallels here with views of Thomas Kuhn (1962) and W.V.O. Quine (1960) on the incommensurability of belief systems, but the main point is that *this* notion of what it is like—which is based on differences between mental economies—is not limited in applicability to other humans and to life-forms entirely alien to ourselves. Indeed, it can, in a very real sense, even apply to ourselves!

The second what-it-is-like notion that Nagel describes has to do with a single 'point of view'. As he says, "every subjective phenomenon is essentially connected with a single point of view, and it seems inevitable that an objective, physical theory will abandon that point of view." (Nagel 220) So this point of view is not capturable by science—at least as we know science today. Perhaps it will in the future? Nagel leaves this possibility open. In science's inability to capture points of view, Nagel feels we are somewhat like the ancient Greeks, who could not comprehend that matter is energy: $E = mc^2$. Even if they could understand the words, they could not comprehend the meanings of the statement.

The third what-it-is-like notion that Nagel describes appears to be *qualia*. Qualia, in this sense, are the felt contents of our sensory experiences: the *blueness* of blue; the *painfulness* of pain, the *sonarness* of sonar. For example, when discussing the bat's experience of sonar, he says "we believe that these [sonar] experiences also have in each case a specific subjective character, which is beyond our ability to conceive." (Nagel 221) Explaining qualia is what the really "hard" problem of consciousness is about. But Nagel seems to be using what-it-is-like not just for qualia, but also for point-of-view and for an agent's mental economy. These are all very different notions, each with its own description and set of problems.

We can now revisit the theme of this essay with regards to Nagel. First, Nagel's what-it-is-like arguments do point out problems with materialism, but, as we have seen, he does not himself take these arguments to be fatal. Second, the main thrust of his arguments in terms of what-it-is-like appear to be focused on internalist conceptions of materialism. Nagel dismisses non-internalist accounts like functionalism as being neobehaviorist, and so lacking in what-it-is-likeness altogether. But third, his notion of what-it-is-like is not a single notion, but rather a collection of three very distinct ideas: the what-it-is-likeness of having a mental economy, having a particular point-of-view, and qualia.

A materialist could perhaps claim that Nagel's arguments critical of materialism based on what-it-is-likeness are ambiguous, and so not as damaging as they might be. But I think the best approach is to recognize, with Feigl (1956), Chalmers (1997) and others, that the third of these notions—qualia—is what poses the real, "hard", challenge to materialism. Given Nagel's arguments, this must mean that qualia must also be lacking entirely in materialist accounts other than internalist accounts—for those other accounts in Nagel's view are neobehaviorist, and neobehaviorism leaves qualia out as a matter of principle, according to him. However, we will see in the final two sections of this paper that this view is mistaken. Externalist accounts of the mind will be shown to account for qualia, while escaping the internalist conceptions and formulations of mind entirely. It's worth noting that even though qualia are perceived as the hard problem of consciousness, Nagel didn't himself take the step of seeing them as a fatal problem for materialism. Kripke and Jackson, on the other hand, do. In this way, we can see that Nagel's recognition of qualia as a problem for materialism set the stage for Kripke's and Jackson's arguments.

2   The Second Dogma: Kripke's modal argument

The second dogma we will consider is Kripke's famous modal argument against materialism. This argument appears in *Naming and Necessity*, where Kripke argues against the identity theory. The identity theory identifies mental states with brain states. Mental states are therefore entirely internal — entirely contained in the head. Kripke's argument is generally accepted to be a powerful argument against materialism about mind. However, we shall see that another form of materialism — externalism — evades his arguments, and indeed actually benefits from Kripke's analysis.

Kripke begins by showing that identities are necessary: if x is identical to y, then necessarily x is identical to y. Further, we can discover some identities *a posteriori*. This means that though it had to be discovered empirically that water is H_2O, it is still a necessary truth that water is H_2O. Hence this is an *a posteriori* necessary truth. This may be all well and good, but what do water and H_2O have to do with the identity theory? The answer is that discussions about water and H_2O have relevance to the identity theory because the claim of mind-brain identity, if it is a strict identity, must also, according to Kripke, be an *a posteriori* identity claim.

How so? Consider the identity 'Pain = C-fiber firing', which we can ascribe to the identity theorist. Presumably this is a scientific identity, and hence discovered *a posteriori*. It should therefore be something like other scientifically discovered identities, such as 'Water = H_2O', and 'Heat = average kinetic energy (KE) of molecules' which, though *a posteriori*, are still necessary. Nevertheless, we appear to be able to imagine pain without C-fiber firings, and vice-versa. If we can really imagine this, doesn't this make 'Pain = C-fiber firing' contingent?

Kripke explains that since all identities are necessary, even *a posteriori* ones, then this incurs an obligation on those who propose an *a posteriori* identity: the obligation of explaining away the appearance of contingency. This can be done, Kripke says, for the two scientific identities mentioned above, 'Water= H_2O', and 'Heat = average KE of molecules'. We will look at each of these in turn below. But it is worth noting a slight difference in these two identities which is important when we are considering theories of mind. The first identity lacks an element of sensation. However, we do sense heat. So understanding the second identity in particular will provide insights into how to account for the contents of sensation with a Kripkean analysis.

How then, do we explain away the illusion of contingency for the first *a posteriori* necessary claim, 'Water is H_2O'? This statement appears contingent, Kripke suggests, because we seem to be able to imagine water that is not H_2O. However, if the identity is necessary, then this can't be what we are imagining. Rather we are really imagining something else, another clear tasteless fluid that quenches thirst, is refreshing to swim in, and so on, but is not H_2O. We are therefore imagining some epistemic counterpart of water. Perhaps there even is such a counterpart substance. But this epistemic counterpart is not water. For water *is* H_2O.

Similarly, Kripke says that since the identity of 'Heat = average KE of molecules' is discovered *a posteriori*, it too will appear contingent. So we must be able to explain away the illusion of contingency. How can we do this? Kripke says:

> When someone says, inaccurately, that heat might have turned out not to be molecular motion, what is true in what he says is that someone could have sensed a phenomenon in the same way we sense heat, that is, feels it by means of its *production of the sensation we call 'the sensation of heat'* (call it '*S*'), even though that phenomenon was not molecular motion. He means, additionally, that the planet might have been inhabited by creatures who did not get *S* when they were in the presence of molecular motion, though perhaps getting it in the presence of something else. Such creatures would be, in some *qualitative* sense, in the same epistemic situation as we are, they could use a rigid designator for the phenomenon that causes sensation *S* in them (the rigid designator could even be 'heat'), yet it would not be molecular motion (and therefore not heat!), which was causing the sensation.(Kripke 1980, p. 150, 151; my italics)

Here, as elsewhere, Kripke is explicitly adopting an internalist picture of sensation. According to this picture, when we refer to the 'sensation of heat'— *S*—we are referring to an *internal quality*—something which is *felt* inside the subject.[1] When we talk of this sensation *S*, we are ***not*** referring to the external molecular motion or Heat, for, as Kripke says above, *S* is "not molecular motion". So *S* can't be Heat, since Heat *is* molecular motion. Further, the sensation *S* is not, it appears, to be identified with a particularly human type of neural structure, or a particularly human type of neural firing, because there could be other creatures with different neural structures from humans who "...were sensitive to that something else, say light, in such a way that they *felt the same thing that we feel* when we feel heat." (Kripke, p. 132; my italics) Again, the 'thing' that is felt here cannot be Heat = average KE of molecules, for if it were, then both these creatures *and* us humans would be feeling the same 'thing' that we feel when we feel heat (viz., Heat = average KE of molecules). But this can't be right, since by assumption these other creatures are responding to light, not Heat. So this 'thing' that is *felt*, by both humans and these other creatures, can only be the sensation *S* - an internal

---

[1] This point is also explicitly made by Kripke: "...it produces in us a sensation of heat"(Kripke, p. 131). In other places he explicitly says "sensations *in* us" and "sensations *in* people" (Kripke, p. 132, and *passim.*)

quality *felt* by us both, despite our being different creatures. Indeed, this is a "*qualitatively* identical epistemic situation."[2] (Kripke, p. 152)

Kripke uses this qualitative approach to sensation to expose the illusion of the contingency of the identity 'Heat = average KE of molecules'. For when these other creatures refer to whatever produces their internal sensations of heat, they are not in fact referring to Heat = average KE of molecules, but to something else, such as light. But we (humans) have already fixed the reference of 'Heat'; it is a rigid designator. Therefore, since 'average KE of molecules' is also a rigid designator and we have discovered that Heat = average KE of molecules, then this identity is necessary. Accordingly, it is just an illusion that those other creatures might be referring to Heat when they have sensations of heat *S*; they are actually referring to something else entirely. The appearance of contingency has been explained away.

I wish to note the importance of what Kripke has just done in the case of heat, since we will be revisiting this example a little later, with regard to other sensory modalities. The point is that Kripke has used Heat - an external property that is not only felt by humans, but that he argues can be rigidly designated by means of an internal indicator state—to establish the illusion of contingency of an empirically discovered *a posteriori identity*. We will find that this sort of argument is a very important one for explaining away the illusion of contingency in other sensory modalities. But first, we should examine Kripke's reply to the identity theorist.

Now let us return to the identity theorist's claim that 'Pain = C-fiber firing'. Kripke says that if this is an *a posteriori* necessary identity, then we must be able to explain away the illusion of contingency. But Kripke says that this move is not possible for the case of 'Pain = C-fiber firing'. According to Kripke, pain is not picked out in the way that heat is, that is, by (the rigidly designated external property) causing us 'feeling the sensation of heat'(Kripke, p. 152). Rather, pain "...is picked out by the property of being pain itself, by its immediate phenomenological quality." (Kripke, p. 152) Thus, any proposed epistemic counterpart of pain, anything that feels like pain, *is* pain. So epistemic counterparts of pain without C-fibers firing will still be pain.

As mentioned earlier, the identities of most interest to the materialist are those which have an experiential (sensational, or felt) component: 'Heat=average KE of molecules' and 'Pain=C-fiber firing'. And Kripke has explained that the first identity holds because what is rigidly designated when we feel the sensation of heat is an external property, Heat, which has been discovered to be identical to the average KE of molecules. In addition, any proposed

---

[2] Perhaps it is also worth noting that that Kripke doesn't say *physically* identical situation here.

epistemic counterparts will not refer to Heat. Yet Kripke tells us that the second identity doesn't hold, because what is rigidly designated when we feel the sensation of pain is an internal sensational quality, pain. Any epistemic counterparts will not be designating something other than pain, but will continue to designate the same quality, pain. Proposed epistemic counterparts therefore also refer to pain.

2.1 Sensations, Obligations, and Feelings

Has materialism been defeated by Kripke's arguments? The answer is no. Kripke's arguments do damage, I believe, to forms of materialism where experiences are taken to be qualities or properties of internal states (in the form in which he sets up the problem), but these arguments entirely miss the mark against, and just do not apply to, externalist formulations of experience.

To show this, let's start by looking carefully at Kripke's analysis of Heat, and the sensing of Heat. The property of Heat that is picked out when we sense Heat, and which is rigidly designated by 'heat' is, Kripke says, outside the head. For the externalist, that is as it should be.

Suppose Jane is by a stream on a sunny spring day. She happens to rest her hand on a dark boulder that has been heated by the sun to 110°. What does she experience in this instance? According to the externalist, she experiences the property of 110°. This is hot, but not uncomfortably so on a spring day. Later, Jane takes off her shoes and wades in the stream. What does she experience in this instance? According to the externalist, she experiences a brisk 45° when she dips her feet in the stream. This is cold, and even makes Jane shiver, despite her being in the sunshine.

Notice that, for the externalist, what is being experienced are physical properties—in this case, the physical temperatures of 110° and 45°—which are external to the head. The contents of our temperature experiences are external to us. But Kripke reminds us that Heat is identical with average KE of molecules, which, as Statistical Mechanics teaches us, is material temperature (Tolman 1956). When, therefore, Jane experiences the physical temperatures of 110° and 45°, she is experiencing Heat. The thoroughly materialist externalist accepts this mandate.

The externalist's formulation of the experience is, however, purely materialistic. What is the experience, for the externalist? It is a relation. The experience is made up of an internal state in the brain, an external property, and the causal relation connecting the two. The internal state has the biological function to indicate (non-conceptually) the external property, under normal conditions where the causal relation holds. (Dretske 1995, Tye 1995, Tye 2000, Skokowski 2002) So in the temperature case we have just considered, what is experienced, what is felt, or what is sensed, when Jane experiences the temperature 110°, is the external property of 110°. This property, 110°, is the content of the experience. Call this property T_{110}. Call the internal state **E**. **E** is caused by T_{110}, and T_{110} is **E**'s content. We are often tempted to call an internal state by itself an experience, but this is too hasty. The internal state **E** is an experiential state, but its content is external. The experience of temperature includes its content, which is the temperature. I will write the experience of T_{110} as **E** (T_{110}). The experiential state **E**, considered by itself, is an internal physical state. It occurs, as neuroscientists tell us, in somatosensory cortex. (Purves 2002, Gazzaniga et al. 2002).

Of course, as we have seen above, this temperature Jane experiences is Heat; she feels the temperature as hotter where the molecules are moving faster, and feels it as cooler where the molecules are moving slower. (Kripke, 129)

The externalist, then, appears to agree with Kripke's analysis of Heat. For we have an external property, such as T_{110}, which causes an internal state **E**. But this isn't quite right. For Kripke's formulation actually is more complex: he adds the additional internal quality of sensation, S. What is felt when Jane touches the rock at T_{110}, according to Kripke, is the sensation S. The quality that Jane experiences, the quality that she feels, when she touches the rock, is not T_{110}, it is the internal quality S.

It might be argued at this point that the internal quality S just is the physical, internal state which I denoted **E**, above. But this is not what Kripke can be intending, for several reasons.

First, sensations and feelings are mental states. Which means that sensations of heat and sensations of pain are mental states. And the whole point of Kripke's argument against the identity "Pain = C-fiber firings" is that mental states may not be physical states. So sensations and feelings, qua mental states, cannot simply be taken to be the internal *physical* states **E** of the externalist picture.[3]

Second, as already noted above, Kripke claims that physically distinct creatures in physically distinct external environments can be in "qualitatively identical epistemic situations". (Kripke, p. 152) These two types of creatures differ in their internal neural structures, and one type is sensitive to an external phenomenon – light – in the same way the other type (presumably human) is sensitive to heat. (Kripke, p. 131,132) But these aren't *physically* identical situations in any manner of speaking: the physical internal neural states *and* the physical external states *and* the causal relationships between the internal and the external states all differ in type here from one creature/environment

---

[3] Note that both pain and heat are *felt* (Kripke, p. 151), and both pain and heat are sensations (Kripke, p. 146 and p. 150).

to the other creature/environment. What remains the same across the two different physical situations are the *qualities*, or *sensations*, or *feelings*, of the creatures. These qualities/sensations/feelings remain the same despite the underlying physical differences. Indeed, Kripke says explicitly that "the sensation of heat ... is an intermediary between the external phenomenon (Heat) and the observer."[4] (Kripke p. 144) This leads to the picture that the observer is the thing with the internal neural state, and the sensation S is the intermediary quality through which the external property Heat is felt, and rigidly designated, by the observer.

Let us compare the externalist's picture for Heat with Kripke's. The externalist says that what I experience when I experience Heat, is the external property T. I am not experiencing some internal property or quality or sensation. Rather, the property I experience is *external* to me. It is a content.[5] For the externalist, the experience of Heat of a particular temperature, say T_{110}, involves an external temperature, T_{110}, *causing* an internal state E. Earlier, I used the notation $E (T_{110})$ to show this relation.

Note that for the externalist, the claim that the phenomenal property (or character) of an experience is the content of the experience is an empirical, *a posteriori*, claim. But other claims, such as water = H_2O, and heat = average kinetic energy of molecules have also been discovered *a posteriori*. If these claims are true, then they are true in all possible worlds. Hence they are *a posteriori* necessary identities. And like these claims, if we discover that the phenomenal property (character) of the experience is the content of the experience, then this will be true in all possible worlds: again, we will have established an *a posteriori* identity. (See also Tye, 1995, 180-195) It is not being assumed that externalism has already been established when considering Kripke's argument. Rather, it is enough to show that externalism is a form of materialism which escapes his argument against materialism. And indeed, as we shall see, externalism escapes Kripke's argument by following and accepting the very prescription that Kripke himself gives for dealing with experiences—and by not only following and accepting this prescription, but also applying it consistently. But first, let us look a little more closely at Kripke's analysis of temperature and heat.

Kripke agrees with the externalist that when we experience temperature T_{110}, there is an external property T_{110}. However, as we have seen, he places the sensation of Heat, S, as an intermediary between the external phenomenon and the observer with her type of neural structure. We have, then, something intermediary—the sensation S—to the observer's neural structure, call it E,

---

[4] It should also be noted that Kripke used dualistic language earlier, p. 145, when he distinguishes between a 'person' (Descartes) and his 'body' B. The latter is physical.

[5] Tye (1995) calls this content a PANIC—a Poised Abstract Nonconceptual Intentional Content.

and the external property **T**. Let us denote Kripke's interpretation of this situation as: **E***S*(**T**). That is, he has inserted an extra, qualitative, property into the relation.

Kripke seems to believe that there are three things going on with respect to the phenomenological aspects of sensing Heat: a neural state, a sensation of Heat, and Heat. For an externalist this is just a confusion. There are only two physical states involved: the external phenomenon of Heat, and the internal sensory state whose biological function it is to indicate Heat. The external state causes the internal state under the right conditions. Since it is the internal state's biological function to indicate this external condition, then we have the required causal connection for the state **E** to rigidly designate Heat. The externalist doesn't need an intermediary feeling between the experiential neural state **E** and Heat. For a particular external token of Heat **T** *causing* the internal state **E** just *is* the experience of **T**.

Is the externalist being disingenuous? Could it be that for Kripke, sensations of heat *S* are really just neural structures? This is not what Kripke is claiming. Recall that the other creatures Kripke says we have imagined (falsely) as sensing heat have differing neural structures from humans, while having the same sensations as humans.[6] (Kripke, 131-133) But if sensations *were* just neural structures, then these creatures *would* have the same neural structures as humans, contrary to what was assumed. This is enough to show that sensations of heat are not neural structures for Kripke. But there are further problems if this assumption were to be pressed. If sensations were neural structures, then because these other creatures have the same sensations =

---

[6] It strikes me, when reading Kripke, that the alternative 'creature' he describes has different types of internal physical states from humans. But if there is a way of reading Kripke differently – that the creature can have the same type of internal state that I do when I experience Heat, and still be experiencing, say, light – the externalist has a reply. We can imagine an individual with a set of identical neurons (in type, not token, of course) in somatosensory cortex to mine. Indeed, when these neurons fire within this creature in exactly the same way as mine fire when I feel Hot = T_{110} degrees, this creature is picking out light, not heat. (We could even think of this as an inversion, say, of two parts of cortex: somatosensory cortex is picking out light for this creature, and 'visual' cortex is picking out Heat.) Perhaps (for historical/linguistic reasons) this creature even says "I'm feeling something Hot right now" when he goes into this state. But, for the externalist, the problem here is that the phenomenological properties of an experience are just the properties of the external phenomenon being experienced. So, if I experience Heat, what is being *experienced* is the property of the external phenomenon which is Heat, and *that* property is avg KE of molecules (a kinetic phenomenon). But when the creature says he is experiencing Heat, what is being *experienced* is the property of the external phenomenon which is light, and *that* property is a wave packet (an electromagnetic phenomenon). So, for the externalist, it is not possible for one to experience (sense, feel) Heat when one is, instead, picking out light in the environment. So, if this is the case Kripke is imagining here, then the externalist says he's wrong about what the creature's quality of experience is: the quality of experience is light, not Heat.

neural structures it would mean that these creatures *would* be able to pick out heat in their environment. Why? Because humans use their sensations=neural structures to pick out heat in their environment. So, by sharing the same sensations of heat as humans—sensations which actually pick out heat in the environment—they also share the same neural structures as humans: neural structures which pick out heat in the environment. Yet the problem was supposed to be that when these creatures have a 'sensation of heat' they are really picking out light in the environment. But human sensations=neural structures of heat are not sensations of light: the two are distinct sensory modalities with distinct causal relations with external properties. For humans, the neural structures that pick out light (neurons in visual cortex) are different from the neural structures that pick out heat (in somatosensory cortex.). (Purves 2003; Zeki 1993; Gazzaniga 2002) There is no overlap. So if the other creatures have the same sensations as humans, as is required for the argument, and these sensations are neural structures, then the creatures will sense heat and light in the same way humans do, and they will not, after all, differ from humans by 'sensing' heat when they in fact are causally 'picking out' light in the environment. Their sensations=neural structures for heat will pick out heat, not light. So the other creatures, who were assumed to differ from humans internally, would not differ. Since this is not the scenario Kripke has drawn for us, sensations cannot be neural structures.

But if sensations are not neural structures, then the externalist sees Kripke as multiplying entities unnecessarily, for internal neural state types (such as are found in somatosensory cortex) which have the biological function of indicating ranges of heat in the environment are what give humans the ability to pick out Heat (of various magnitudes) in the world in the first place. These types of states were selected because they could reliably pick out certain physical properties crucial to survival in the environment. Thus it is biological function which provides the sensory foundation for picking out properties in the environment, and hence for rigid designation of these properties. The externalist can therefore apply Occam's razor and get rid of the dangler—the *intermediary* sensation/feeling/quality—for the sensation is seen to just be the heat causing the internal state, and nothing more (Skokowski 2002, 2003). What is the quality of the heat being experienced? It is the Heat, the temperature T, in the environment: this is the content of the experience. The heat being felt is the actual heat. There is no need for an extra quality of the *feeling* of heat to be added in to the formula.

Heat is therefore picked out by its actual physical properties. Thus the externalist's formulation of materialism denies Kripke's assumption that there can be creatures that, for example, sense (experience) light in the same way humans sense (experience) Heat. The reason is that the contents of the sensations comprise the qualities of the sensations. And the contents of the sensations, for externalists, are exhausted by the physical property or properties of the phenomenon sensed (experienced, felt). Therefore a creature that senses light (via visual cortex), is experiencing light; this creature is not experiencing heat. There are no properties of heat (considered as material temperature, a kinetic phenomenon) that are shared with light (an electromagnetic phenomenon). Similarly, a creature that senses heat (via somatosensory cortex) is not experiencing light. And since the contents differ in physical properties, there is no way in which the two creatures' experiences are the same.

Kripke's analysis of sensing heat has therefore turned out to benefit the externalist. For humans do indeed pick out the external property of heat, and the causal interaction which picks heat out is what underlies rigid designation of the property heat. But the externalist holds that heat is picked out by states in somatosensory cortex (that is the function of these states), not by extra 'feelings' inserted between the internal state and the external property. And so the externalist has a purely materialist formulation of rigid designation of this external property, with exactly the physical machinery on offer.

How does the externalist deal with the obligation of explaining away the illusion of contingency of 'Pain=C-fiber firings'? There is a short answer: the externalist doesn't have an obligation to explain it at all, because the externalist denies the identity. Pain isn't to be identified with firing properties of C-fibers, because pain isn't a property of Jane's brain. Instead, pain experiences (or pain sensations, or pain feelings) have bodily disturbances (cuts, burns, bruises, etc.) as their experienced properties, together with types of internal states (perhaps C-fiber firings) that have the biological function (conferred by natural selection) to indicate these properties under optimal conditions, and causal relations that connect the two types of states. The externalist holds that these bodily disturbances are (with the exceptions of headaches, etc.) external to the brain. The properties of these disturbances are taken to be contents for the experience of pain analogously to how various magnitudes for Heat are contents for the experience of heat. Let me refer to the properties of these bodily disturbances as 'painful properties'. These properties—for example, 'stabbing pain in Jane's right foot', 'burning pain in Jane's left thumb', 'throbbing pain in Jane's right ankle', and so on—are physical properties of Jane's bodily disturbances: disturbances—such as the puncture of stepping on a nail with her right foot, the burned flesh of touching her left thumb to the pan on the stove, or the cartilage tears and swelling of having a twisted right ankle—which the externalist holds are the contents of Jane's pain experiences.[7] And these painful properties are (generally) external to Jane's head.

But now the reply will surely be that 'painful properties = bodily disturbances' appears contingent. So the externalist now has the obligation to explain away this appearance of contingency. And how can the externalist do that? As was mentioned earlier, Kripke has already provided us a prescription for doing this: We can explain the illusion of contingency in the same way that the illusion of contingency of 'Heat = average KE of molecules' was dealt with earlier. For an externalist formulation of materialism, painful properties are external to the head in the same way that heat is external to the head; nevertheless, both are experienced as contents. Thus under this formulation of materialism, both contents can be treated in the same way. And Kripke has given us a way to deal with the apparent contingency of experiences of heat. Recall that Kripke said that in such cases we seemed to be imagining creatures and environments different from us that experienced/sensed/felt the same thing as humans did. Analogously, it appears that we can imagine creatures that differ from humans in their physical structure, evolutionary history, and environment, that experience painful properties. We are imagining, then, that such creatures have internal states which indicate external conditions in their environment, perhaps even in their 'bodies', and could even say 'I am experiencing pain' when this occurs. But when these other creatures refer to whatever external properties cause their internal states, they are not in fact referring to physical properties of the type that constitute painful properties. Note that it makes no difference whether or not these creatures' internal states might be referring to a disturbance inside their bodies. For by hypothesis, the internal and external physical *properties* must be different in physical type for this creature and its environment when it experiences pain from the human's internal and external physical properties, and so therefore, must be the causal law connecting the two, and the selection history of this type of internal state must also be completely different from the human case. Indeed, by hypothesis, the 'bodily disturbances' of the creature are of a completely different physical type from a human's bodily disturbances in an analogous way to how properties of light are of a completely different physical type from properties of heat. But, just as Kripke pointed out for 'heat', we (humans) have already fixed the reference of 'painful properties'; it is a rigid designator of the kinds of bodily disturbances that happen to humans (and possibly other animals) on our planet. So when these other creatures refer to whatever produces their internal states, they are not in fact referring to what we have rigidly designated to be painful properties, but to something else entirely. So what we have really managed to imagine is something different from our

---

[7] Note that in Tye's (1995) formulation, painful properties would be PANICs.

experience of pain.[8] It is therefore just an illusion that those other creatures might be referring to painful properties; they are referring to other physical properties entirely. The appearance of contingency has been explained away.

But surely, it will be replied, pain is a special case. Pain is different from heat. For Kripke says that heat is picked out by virtue of the fact that heat produces the sensation of heat within us. However, Kripke says that Pain is not picked out by producing a painful sensation in us, but rather by its immediate phenomenological property. Anything that feels like a pain is a pain. And Kripke has argued, through considering non-human creatures, that not everything that feels like heat, is heat.

But the externalist has a reply: pain sensations/experiences/feelings *are* like heat sensations/experiences/feelings. For all sensations—pain included—involve internal states which have the function of indicating external properties—properties appropriate for that sense modality. Pain, therefore, is not a special case for the externalist formulation of materialism in the way Kripke wants it to be. Indeed, we need only to look at how another external physical quality—that of heat—can be sensed according to his model, in order to proceed in a consistent fashion to a general externalist model of sensation.

The externalist can even agree with Kripke on a further point: that not everything that feels like heat is heat. But that is because the senses, being representational in nature, have the ability to *mis*-represent their surroundings: they have the ability, that is, to be wrong. Misrepresentation is always possible for biological systems. (Dretske 1988; Dretske 1995; Tye 1995; Skokowski 2000; Skokowski 2004) I can touch the ice and 'feel' it as hot. This is a misrepresentation. I can 'see' the yellowy-orange afterimage even though nothing in my vicinity is yellowy-orange. This is a misrepresentation. I can 'hear' a ringing in my ears after a severe ear infection even though there is no ringing. This is a misrepresentation. Why should pain be any different? I can recall 'feeling' pain when I dreamed I twisted my ankle. But there was no pain. This was a misrepresentation. Amputees can feel 'phantom' pains.

---

[8] Note that Putnamian (1968) arguments about Martians won't work against the externalist. The reason is that our pain experiential states have a biological function: that function is to indicate physical disturbances in bodies of a certain type (presumably bodies in this world are carbon-based). The history we have in our world has selected these kinds of states to do this job. Martians have a different biological history and hence will have a different function: theirs will indicate (presumably) silicon disturbances. Since history determines function, that is, function is conferred by natural selection, then different histories will yield different functions. Putnam's arguments (1968) do not address these differences. For the externalist, such histories are crucial. See Dretske 1988, 1995, Tye 1995, Skokowski 2004.

These are misrepresentations of (non-existent) bodily disturbances. That is why we refer to them as 'phantom' pains, and not actual pains.

It is not an objection to the externalist to point out that sensory systems misrepresent; indeed, it is a *strength* of the externalist formulation of mind that it can *explain* misrepresentation in naturalistic terms (see Dretske 1988; Dretske 1995; Tye 1995; Tye 2000; Skokowski 2004; Skokowski 2018.) The biological function of our internal sensory detectors (for example, detection of heat by somatosensory cortex and detection of visual properties by visual cortex) is derived from our evolutionary history. These detectors have been given a job to do by natural selection. When they go awry, which can happen for biological systems, then they can misrepresent. Kripke has, after all, used these same faulty systems to provide the very mechanisms relied upon to rigidly designate certain properties in the environment—properties that are sometimes *mis*represented by the very same faculties. So occasional misrepresentation does not incriminate sensory modalities, or keep them from picking out their appropriate physical properties when optimal conditions obtain; rather, sensory misrepresentation should be explained naturalistically, something that the externalist actually does. But Kripke offers no explanation of misrepresentation.

So for the externalist, not everything that feels like heat is heat. And similarly, not everything that feels like a painful property is a painful property. Misrepresentation is not only possible, but it occurs in every sensory modality at various times.

2.2 Assumptions and Intuitions

A possible reply to this could be that, 'In order to explain the apparent contingency, Kripke says it would help if one could point to the real possibility of someone to whom something other than pain appears just as pain appears to me, because that would give a real sense in which all my evidence prior to doing neuroscience was compatible with it turning out that with "pain" I was referring to something other than what actually *is* pain. That's the model that he takes to work fine with "Heat = average KE of molecules". There, a pre-scientific me is matched by a really possible individual who has the same evidence in every internally noticeable sense and yet who refers with "heat" to something other than Heat.'[9]

But here, says the externalist, is precisely the problem. As is pointed out above, what is important for Kripke is 'evidence in every internally noticeable sense.' But this is an assumption on Kripke's part: namely, that all the evidence available is internal evidence. Yet Kripke nowhere gives an

---

[9] I owe this way of putting the objection to Mark Crimmins.

argument to support this assumption. Instead, he wants us to simply accept the intuition that sensations—the qualities of experience—are purely internal. And if sensations are internal, then giving individuals the same type of sensations seems to allow that they are both sensing heat regardless of the external environment.[10] But the externalist does not accept this intuition. Instead, he offers a different intuition: the evidence is actually external, because the qualities of experience are external. And if the evidence is external, this places the evidence in the world. If we put the evidence in the world, then it will be the external content of the experience which will determine legitimate cases of really possible individuals who are experiencing Heat (or painful properties, or...). And what is all the evidence prior to neuroscience? Consider the fact that there are other pre-scientific, pre-theoretical individuals: children. Ask a child where the yellow is when she looks at a daffodil. She will reply 'on the daffodil'. Ask a child where it hurts after she falls on the pavement. She will say 'my knee'. Ask the child what is hot after she touches the stove. She will say 'the stove'. These are equally applicable, and equally plausible, pre-theoretic, pre-scientific intuitions. And these are intuitions which differ from Kripke's. These intuitions place the felt quality of experience external to the head, and in the world. And is it just children who hold such intuitions? Surely there are also many adults who hold identical pre-theoretic, pre-scientific intuitions.[11] So the externalist denies the intuition that what is sensed is 'internally noticeable.' Instead, the externalist says it is at least an equally plausible intuition that the property experienced is external. So Kripke's model of inserting a sensation internally, or as an intermediary between the agent and the property felt (heat) is rejected. Kripke doesn't have the right to simply impose his intuitions across the board. His assumption needs to be supported by a further argument that shows that his intuition is the only acceptable one.

The externalist will therefore reject Kripke's explanation of contingency for heat. For Kripke's explanation depends on the assumption that an internal sensation—the quality of experience—is being caused by an external property (Heat). The sensation is an internal quality that is intermediary between the observer and the external property. The externalist says that this model is flawed and so another explanation must be given. The externalist proposes an alternative causal explanation of the experience of heat: that an internal state (in somatosensory cortex, for example) is what is caused by the external property (heat). Further, the external property is the quality of the sensation:

---

[10] As mentioned above, Dretske (1995) calls this assumption that sensations are entirely internal the 'internalist intuition'.

[11] Perhaps, in some cases, our thinking becomes infected with the internalist intuition only after studying certain philosophers; for example, Berkeley or Hume!

this quality is the content of sensation—a property that is in the world, not in the head. The Kripkean move of inserting a 'sensation' S in addition to the external property and the observer creates, as Jackson (1982) has put it in a related context, an excrescence: the 'sensations' S are epiphenomena that seem to be inserted precisely to satisfy the internalist intuition that sensations are somehow internal.

But despite rejecting Kripke's version of the explanation of the contingency, the externalist can still successfully explain the mechanism that underlies rigid designation: the picking out of the external property by an internal state. For the externalist this internal state is a neural state (type) which has the biological function of picking out that property in the environment. And nature has provided precisely such mechanisms for picking out these very properties: mechanisms in visual cortex that pick out visual contents, mechanisms in somatosensory cortex that pick out heat contents, etc. No extra internal sensory qualities are required for these mechanisms. The externalist claims that his explanation of 'picking out' properties in the world is ontologically simpler than Kripke's, using only extant physical properties and causal relations, and is ultimately more satisfying given the success of materialistic scientific accounts.

So the externalist rejects Kripke's intuition that sensations/feelings/experiences are entirely internal. And this leads him to reject Kripke's explanation of contingency.

There is another problem with Kripke's claim that pain is not picked out by producing a painful sensation, but rather by its immediate phenomenological property that I will mention briefly here before concluding. The problem is that Kripke never actually proves this assertion. Instead, the externalist sees this claim as an assumption on Kripke's part, an assumption that he is not entitled to. The externalist has given a separate (non-identity theory) formulation of materialism that Kripke's attack on the identity theory does not— and, as has been argued above, cannot—eliminate. Kripke has not considered the case that pain experiences include a physical content of the experience; something we have called here a 'painful property', which is external to the head. Indeed, for the externalist, pain experiences *do* require occurrent 'painful properties', but these external painful properties go on to *cause* internal states—states which are not themselves exemplifying these painful properties. It is not the internal states which exhibit these painful properties; these properties are external to the head. So for the externalist, painful properties *are* picked out by producing an internal state, but the internal state isn't the pain, and the pain is not a property of this internal state. The externalist's version of events is just as immediate (in a temporal, as opposed to a spatial, sense), however, and has all the painful properties required of pain, but pain just isn't an internal property, and it certainly isn't a non-physical property.

To Kripke's question "Do you find it at all plausible that that very sensation could have existed without being a sensation, the way a certain inventor (Franklin) could have existed without being an inventor?" (Kripke, 146), the answer is 'Yes and No'. *Yes*, those very neurons could have existed (in that firing state) without their firing in response to painful properties, and *Yes*, that bodily disturbance could have occurred without being the painful property (anaesthesia, damaged nerves, different wiring, etc.). But for the experience writ large, that is, the internal experiential state (whose function has been determined by its evolutionary history) which indicates an external content (under optimal conditions), the answer is: *No*, it could not have existed without being that experience.

Kripke's argument against the identity theory is a powerful argument against one form of materialism, the identity theory. But by failing to consider that the contents of our experiences can be external to our heads, Kripke's argument misses another form of materialism entirely: externalism. Indeed, the externalist analysis of rigid designation offers an improved formulation of the causal basis of how sensory systems pick out their properties in the environment: a formulation that avoids inserting extra 'feelings' between internal neural states and the external properties these states have the function of indicating.

3   The Third Dogma: Jackson's Knowledge Argument

The third dogma is Frank Jackson's knowledge argument. We will see that while this argument poses a formidable hurdle for internalist accounts of materialism, it fails against externalist accounts. The argument begins by describing a special subject, Mary, who has lived her entire life in a black and white room. She is a brilliant neuroscientist who knows everything physical there is to know, through reading black and white books, watching lectures on black and white screens, and so on. However, despite this colossal amount of knowledge, it appears there is some knowledge that Mary lacks. For it seems obvious that when she first emerges from her room and sees a red rose, she will for the first time *experience* red, and this experience will be a kind of knowledge that until that moment she lacked. But Mary already *had* all the physical knowledge, so this new knowledge is non-physical.

The knowledge argument can be stated simply:

(1) Mary has all the physical knowledge at time *t*.

(2) Mary gains new knowledge at *t* + *dt*.

Therefore:

There is knowledge that escapes materialism, and so is nonphysical.

But the knowledge argument relies on an assumption, which is also simply stated:

(3) Mary can *have* all the physical knowledge while being confined to her room.

But if this assumption (3) is false, then the knowledge argument fails. That is, if Mary *cannot have all the physical knowledge* while being confined to her room, then knowledge she gains when leaving the room may be physical knowledge after all. As Jackson himself says, "What she knows beforehand [in her room] is ex hypothesi everything physical there is to know", (Jackson 1985, p. 292) which makes assumption (3) explicit. We will see that this assumption can be denied through a failure to recognize an alternative formulation of materialism: externalism. The conclusion, then, does not follow.[12]

This assumption is a legitimate target for materialism. And in particular, externalism has the apparatus to show how this assumption fails to hold for the kinds of knowledge at issue in the argument.[13]

Under Jackson's formulation, to have knowledge about some properties, states, processes, and so on, means that one has information about those properties, states, and processes. (Jackson 1982) When Mary leaves her room and experiences red for the first time, she learns something about the world. Her experience delivers phenomenal information—qualia (colors, tastes, etc.)— through the senses. As Jackson puts it, these "qualia are left out of the physicalist story." (Jackson 1982, 130) These qualia are therefore not physical. For Jackson, the strength of the knowledge argument "...is that it is so hard to deny the central claim that one can have all the physical information *without having all the information there is to have*." (Jackson 1982, 130) This

---

[12] It is worth noting that Jackson (2003, 2006) has recently joined the materialist camp.

[13] I will follow Jackson (2003) in using materialism and physicalism interchangeably, and in construing materialism about mind as holding that "...the mind is a purely physical part of a purely physical world." (Jackson 2003, p. 251)

means that the information delivered by our experiences—the contents, or qualia—is not physical information. Such nonphysical knowledge or nonphysical information 'escapes the physical story'. (Jackson 1982, p. 130; Jackson 1985, p. 293) This sort of information will include not just colors like red, but also sounds, bodily sensations, tastes, and so on. (Jackson 1982, p. 129, 130) These are all qualia. I will denote experiences which have this sort of content "**E**"—experiences of qualia. We can also assume, along with Jackson, knowledge that is not experiential, such as knowledge that 2 x 3 = 6, knowledge that Macron is president of France, or knowledge that Mary has neural state N at time t. I will designate by "**K**" knowledge states that are not experiential. Physical information need not only involve particular properties and states, but also can involve interrelations. These interrelations can involve tokens (brain state X is related to some external state Y—the state of a rose, say), but can also involve types, as is the case for physical laws (physical state X causes physical state Y under background conditions Z.)[14]

The problem for the knowledge argument is that materialism recognizes Mary's physical limitations of confinement within her room precisely *as* physical limitations. When Mary is physically enclosed, she is being isolated from direct experiences of certain physical properties in the world, and this isolation will prevent some knowledge of the physical world. For internalist forms of materialism this poses an immediate problem.[15] For an internalist materialist, all knowledge is physical and is contained inside the head. Surely Mary must already know about red before exiting the room, for all knowledge is physical and so must already be *in her head*. But it seems inescapable that something novel is experienced by Mary upon her exit, and so she will gain new, incremental, information and knowledge about red at the instant she steps outside. This is a predicament for internalism: even though Mary has all the physical knowledge within her head of the color red while in the room, she still obtains new knowledge of red upon going outside.

But materialism is not limited to an internalist interpretation. For an externalist, colors can be taken to be properties of physical objects which are outside of the head. Since for a materialist all knowledge is physical, an externalist can maintain that certain kinds of physical knowledge are denied to Mary from the peculiar, physical, limitations of her confinement. Such physical limitations have the consequence that Mary *cannot* have all the physical

---

[14] See Kim (1973), Mackie (1974), and Goldman (1970) for causal and event type/token formalizations.

[15] Perry (2001), to give one example, gives a strong case for saving internalist-style materialism from Jackson's argument.

knowledge while being restricted to her room.[16] Thus assumption (3) is false, or at a minimum demands further argument, and either suffices to make the knowledge argument, as it stands, fail.

It is important to note that one does not need to establish materialism in order to overcome the knowledge argument. All that is required is to show a form of materialism which the knowledge argument does not address. That is what the arguments that follow will establish. We will see that the knowledge argument has a restricted applicability to internalism, and misses externalism entirely.[17]

It is clear that when Mary exits her room, she learns something. Jackson says Mary gains knowledge "about the world and our visual experience of it." (Jackson 1982, 130). Jackson says Mary in addition obtains knowledge about other people. (Jackson 1985, 293) Jackson has already established that some qualia—in this instance, Red qualia—are not included in Mary's physical knowledge prior to leaving the room. So we know at the very least, that Mary will gain knowledge that a person P experiences the quale R (Red) when first seeing a red rose. In this way Mary gains knowledge of other people, which is part of Jackson's point. But it is also evident that when Mary steps outside the room at $t + dt$, she obtains the knowledge that *she* experiences R when seeing the red rose.[18] Both are uncontroversial, given that Mary learns something when she leaves the room, and that what she learns about include '...mental states which are said to have...qualia.'(Jackson, 1982 p. 130) I will follow standard usage and call such mental states experiences or sensations.

Now it is worth asking the question of whether these experiences or sensations—for example the experience of (the quale) R—are themselves a kind of knowledge? This seems plausible, as Mary undeniably experiences Red at $t + dt$ for the first time. Mary here gains a novel experience of a new quale R. But, as will see in a following section, experiential states differ from knowledge states in vehicle, content and causal role. Details for these differences will be given later, but an important distinction we can recognize now is that for an externalist, experiences are internal states that directly and causally co-vary with an external property. This property is the content of the

---

[16] There are others who have argued to the effect that Mary does not have all the physical knowledge (see, for example, Stoljar 2001 and Horgan 1984), but their arguments are not from the viewpoint of externalism, as defended here.

[17] In externalism, contents of mental states will be (typically) outside the head. See for example, Dretske (1988, 1995), Tye (1995), Skokowski (2007).

[18] Tye (2009, 133) and Crane (2012, 196) say that Mary learns 'that this is what it is like to experience red.' Either usage works for the purposes of this section, and either will, given the examples in subsequent sections, count as new physical knowledge that Mary gains when she leaves the room.

experience, and is not what we would generally say is the content of a that-clause; in other words, this property is not taken to be propositional. Following the accounts of Dretske (1990, 1995) and Crane (2012) on simple seeing, we can say that when Mary exits the room she will be 'seeing Red' or 'experiencing Red' for the first time. Such non-propositional mental states are quite familiar for philosophical and psychological usage[19] (Crane 2012; Dretske 1990; Dretske 1995), which brings up a technicality: must all the knowledge gained by Mary when she leaves the room be propositional?

I think it's fair to say that when Mary first experiences Red, that the experiencing itself counts as something Mary learns, and so counts as a kind of knowledge. But a knowledge purist might counter that non-propositional knowledge doesn't count. Given this perspective, experience of Red *simpliciter* won't be knowledge. However, when Mary learns at $t + dt$ that she experiences Red, and when she learns that other people have experienced Red, both will count as knowledge: knowledge that Mary experiences Red upon exiting the room, and knowledge that other people have experienced Red.

There are arguments on both sides on whether an experience should be considered as knowledge. I believe it should count. But it will transpire that in either case, the knowledge argument fails against externalism. Let's begin by considering temperature.

3.1 Temperature

We now revisit Mary in a slightly different black and white room. This room is always kept to a constant temperature of 98.6 degrees. Further, any item that is placed in the room is at this temperature or higher. Mary loves black coffee, and sometimes the coffee overheats and scalds her tongue. If the coffee is left out, it will shortly equilibrate to 98.6 degrees. Of course, though being restricted to her room, Mary knows all this, of course, since she knows everything there is to know about thermodynamics and neuroscience.

When it comes to feeling 98.6 degrees, Mary knows what it is like. Every day. The room is in equilibrium, and the surfaces, walls, and most other objects in the room are at this temperature. But Mary also knows what 180 degrees is like, as that is the coffee's temperature when she tastes it freshly poured in her cup. She also knows what 130 degrees is like, which is the temperature her black and white computer attains a few hours after being

---

[19] Crane (2012) also makes the point that this familiar notion of seeing can be used without any need to invoke a Russellian notion of acquaintance in addressing the knowledge argument. I think this is right, and furthermore, that an externalist accounting of knowledge and experience (which includes 'seeing') will be enough to show how the knowledge argument fails against externalism.

switched on. It's fair to say that Mary knows a range of temperatures from 98.6 upwards.

One day, Mary is allowed enter an adjacent room, which is also, it turns out, black and white. However this room has a difference: it is kept at 30 degrees. What happens when Mary enters this new room? As Jackson puts it, 'it seems just obvious that she will learn something'. Mary will now learn what it is like to be 30 degrees, and thus, what it is like to be COLD. Her knowledge is, therefore, incomplete. However, Mary has all the physical knowledge. So this is nonphysical knowledge.

By every account, Mary is an especially brilliant scientist. And so it is particularly intriguing that, with everything she knows about thermodynamics and temperature, she is nevertheless surprised to find that she has learned something, and in particular something non-physical, upon entering the new room. Would an externalist (and, for that matter, Mary) agree?

Mary's background in neuroscience means she knows about specialized detectors—nerves at the extremities—with the function to detect temperatures. Indeed, Mary recognizes that when she experiences an object's temperature, *what* she experiences, the *content* of her experience, is the temperature of the object. This she recognizes as an instantiation of a physical law: When objects of (temperature-) type T are brought into contact with her extremities, then this contact causes an event in her brain—neural activations in somatosensory cortex—of type E. (Gazzaniga et al. 2002; Purves et al., 2002)

Mary will know, for example, that objects with temperatures (such as 30 degrees F), and experiential states (such as a specific collection of neurons firing within somatosensory cortex) are physical states. Their physical properties are instances of types, which physicists and neuroscientists would refer to as *Temperature* and *Sensory Neural Firing*. These types are connected through physical laws (Kim 1973). Various instances of these physical laws are examined and substantiated in laboratories. For example, when an object with a temperature of 500 degrees F is brought into contact with Mary's hand, she will quickly withdraw it. This temperature causes a brain event, which in turn causes activations in motor neurons, with the result that Mary rapidly withdraws her hand from the object. Mary knows all this.

Mary will also know (as will an externalist) that in the unfortunate event of her experiencing 500 degrees, nothing in her brain will be 500 degrees. And in particular, the state E occurring in her somatosensory cortex will not be 500 degrees. Mary knows that it is the external object which exemplifies that property.

Consider now a completely material, physical, theory of temperature and the sensing of temperature. Given this view, temperatures are exhibited as properties of objects, experiential states are instantiated in brains, and certain experiential states will have the natural function of indicating temperatures. The latter have the job of indicating temperatures—a job conferred by natural selection. Under this picture, an experience of a temperature will involve a relation between a (temperature) property of an external object and a (firing) property of a state in the brain. It turns out that externalists choose this kind of physical explanation as the best one on offer (Dretske 1995; Tye 1995, 2000).

Nobody can prevent Mary from holding such a view, so let's suppose for a moment that Mary holds such a view. Nothing in the arguments that follow require that Mary holds this view. But it is not unreasonable to suppose Mary to be a materialist who fully expects to gain new, physical, knowledge upon exiting her room. Of course, what makes this particularly interesting in Mary's case, is that if she indeed holds such a view, then she will *expect* to learn something new in the new room. Surely Mary, given her prodigious knowledge, expects to gain the experience of a new property soon after opening the door. And this would mean that she comprehends beforehand that she does not have all the physical knowledge during her confinement.

Recall that, according to the knowledge argument, Mary will acquire new information through such an experience, and 'she will learn something about the world'. (Jackson 1982, p. 130) Mary knows what 98.6 degrees and 500 degrees are like through her previous experiences of these (and other) temperatures. Mary therefore has internal experiential states of type E, that covary with temperatures T, in such a way that states of type E indicate, or carry information on temperatures T. Mary's *experience* of 500 degrees carries the *information* 500 degrees. (Dretske 1995) We will write this relation as $E(500)$, which stands for a token with property temperature $T=500$ degrees causing a neural state E, with E carrying information $T=500$ degrees. More generally we will write $E(T)$, for arbitrary temperatures T.

After exiting the room, Mary experiences 30 degrees, exemplifying the relation $E(30)$. She thereby gains information 30 degrees according to Jackson's prescription, by directly experiencing that temperature. Jackson tells us this new information is a quale—the content of a bodily sensation—and therefore is non-physical. An externalist will agree with Jackson about the new information, but she will disagree that this information is non-physical.

All experience is physical for an externalist. Both the *vehicle* of the experience—the internal neural state E—and the *content* of the experience—the external physical property T—are physical. Moreover, the two states will be bound together through a nomic regularity, a regularity which underlies the attribution of informational content. However, Mary will not have the information if either the vehicle or content is absent. John can't have the information that the Avon lady is on his porch if the Avon lady is not on his porch.

Here information is precluded because there is no content. Further, John cannot have the information the Avon lady is on his porch if John is at the farmers' market without his cell phone, even if the Avon lady is on his front porch. In this case information is precluded because the vehicle is lacking.

Note that Mary lacks *both* the vehicle E *and* the content 30 degrees before she enters the new room. This denies her the physical experience $E(30)$. But immediately upon stepping through the door she will experience a temperature of 30 degrees. Mary now has the *physical experience* $E(30)$, which her previous confinement denied her. This is not an experience with a non-physical content: 30 degrees is a physical property—also known as material temperature. (Tolman 1956) 30 degrees is neither non-physical information nor is it a non-physical property. It is a physical property in the natural world.

A response to this might be, "Although there will be no *experience* of 30 degrees before Mary leaves the room, nevertheless she could *know* about 30 degrees in other ways. She could have studied fMRI scans of subjects who are experiencing 30 degrees, and she could also examine people who are experiencing 30 degrees in a variety of other ways. So before ever leaving the room she could have all the physical information about 30 degrees."

An externalist will not dispute that a certain sort of knowledge is available to Mary before she leaves the room. But this knowledge differs in vehicle, content, and causal role, and so is a very different kind of knowledge. Moreover, the knowledge and experience which are at issue are denied to Mary by virtue of her physical confinement.[20] Let us consider these differences in detail.

Suppose Mary observes John (via black and white streaming) while he is experiencing 30 degrees. Here, Mary will definitely have a knowledge state, according to externalism. This knowledge state will include a neural state, which we'll call K^{Mary} (where the superscript 'Mary' specifies that this internal state belongs to Mary), whose content is John's neural state, which consists of John's experiential state, call it E^{John}, and the temperature he experiences, 30 degrees, which is itself the content of John's internal experiential state E^{John}. We can write Mary's knowledge that John is experiencing 30 degrees as: $K^{Mary} [E^{John} (30 \text{ degrees})]$. This denotes that Mary's internal knowledge state K^{Mary} has the content $E^{John} (30 \text{ degrees})$.

But now note that Mary will understand that her *knowledge* that John is experiencing 30 degrees is different altogether from her own *experience* of 30 degrees. As a brilliant neuroscientist, Mary already knows that her

---

[20] Alter (2013, 492) makes a similar point: Mary "…cannot arrive at the relevant phenomenal knowledge$_M$ by deducing truths from her knowledge$_M$ of the complete physical truth and her knowledge$_P$ of phenomenal truths about what it is like to see in colour." What Alter calls knowledge$_P$ is the knowledge Mary has of others' color experiences before she leaves her room.

knowledge states of the experiences of others will be completely distinct from her own sensory experiences. Applying the same formalism, Mary knows that her knowledge state (of John) is not the same as her own experiential state (of 30 degrees)— that is, $\mathbf{K}^{Mary}[\mathbf{E}^{John}(30\text{ degrees})] \neq \mathbf{E}^{Mary}(30\text{ degrees})$. In what way could they ever have been the same? It is evident that John and Mary are distinct individuals, and so they will have distinct vehicles exemplified in their respective brains (Mary's neural state $\mathbf{K}^{Mary} \neq$ John's neural state $\mathbf{E}^{John}$), but it's also clear that the *contents* of the two types of knowledge are altogether distinct. Mary's knowledge state has as its content John experiencing 30 degrees, which involves a state in John's brain. But the content of Mary's experience of 30 degrees is just the temperature 30 degrees, and this doesn't have anything to do with John whatsoever. So the contents *and* the vehicles differ for the two types of states.

Earlier we saw that what Mary learns upon leaving the room is what it is to *experience* 30 degrees. And *this* instance of learning will include an instantiation of the direct experience of that temperature, that is: $\mathbf{E}^{Mary}(30\text{ degrees})$. Mary will not exemplify that vehicle and experiential content until after she steps into the new room, according to the externalist. The externalist also apprehends that Mary's *knowledge* of 30 degrees through means distinct from direct experience of the temperature—such as obtaining knowledge through her black and white computer—is in no way equivalent to her *experience* of 30 degrees. Once again, the two vehicles $\mathbf{K}$ and $\mathbf{E}$ are entirely different internal neural states, with distinct etiologies, locations, firing frequencies, and so on. Moreover, these states are not only distinct internal vehicle *tokens*, but they are also distinct *types*. An experiential state type like $\mathbf{E}$ is related to temperatures $\mathbf{T}$ through a particular sensory modality, and experiential tokens like $\mathbf{E}$ are themselves caused by an external property (tokening) of 30 degrees. On the other hand, a knowledge type such as $\mathbf{K}$ will be installed over time through a learning history, and the internal neural state $\mathbf{K}$ will *not* be directly caused by a token $\mathbf{T}$ of 30 degrees, but rather will be installed by a history of interactions, including with lecturers who talk about $\mathbf{T}$, with devices that measure $\mathbf{T}$, with course books containing blackbody curves for $\mathbf{T}$, etc.[21] Experiential and knowledge states, therefore, occur in different regions of the brain, and are caused in radically different ways.

Further, the causal consequences of these vehicles are also distinct. One type of state might cause Mary to withdraw her hands, whereas the other will instead cause subsequent thoughts in Mary, or cause her to make certain

---

[21] For learning histories see Dretske (1988). For historical differences between experience and cognitive states see Dretske (1995). For changes through learning in neural substrates see Skokowski (2004).

statements ('exhibits a blackbody curve maximum at …'). The two neuron states of type **E** and **K** have different locations in the brain, as will be apparent both to the neuroscientist Mary, and to an externalist. So it is not just the vehicles which differ, but also the causal roles for these vehicles which differ – both the kinds of events which produce these states, and the kinds of events which are caused by them, are distinct, each from the other.

One might respond that Mary already has all the physical knowledge before she exits the room, including, say, a knowledge state **K** about 30 degrees. But Mary and the externalist would beg to differ. The reason is that Mary already has experience and knowledge of other physical temperature properties, for example, 98.6 degrees, 170 degrees, 500 degrees, and so on. And not only that, she grasps that *knowledge* of these temperatures is different in type from *experiences* of any of them. An illustration of the former is when Mary conceives of the blackbody curve for an object at 170 degrees. She might even say, "When directly experiencing 170 degrees, it *feels* completely different from any knowledge states I have of that temperature. Being a neuroscientist, I realize that when *feeling* 170 degrees, detectors on my periphery cause activity in my somatosensory cortex, whereas when I *think* about 170 degrees, a separate and distinct group of neurons fires elsewhere in my brain. These two collections of neurons—which comprise an experiential state **E**, and a knowledge (thought) state **K**—are completely different from one another, both in their neural vehicles and in their causal relations with other physiological and external states. Therefore, before I exit the room, I understand that any experience of 30 degrees for me will differ from my knowledge of 30 degrees, comparably to how my previous experiences of temperatures differed from my knowledge states of those temperatures. However, before I step out the door, any experience of 30 degrees, **E**(30 degrees), is forbidden to me by my physical restrictions. These restrictions forbid me the physical vehicle **E** for the experience, and prevent the external physical relations required to cause that state in my brain. These physical restrictions therefore deny me *this* kind of experience and physical knowledge." Therefore, despite allowing that Mary (before exiting the room) knows (**K**) about 30 degrees, we also see that she will know that she *lacks* any *experience* **E** of 30 degrees. And not only that, Mary also understands that she lacks direct knowledge of this experience K^{Mary} [E^{Mary} (30 degrees)], for a knowledge state of this type cannot be exemplified until *after* she exits the room.[22] So, contrary to assumptions of the knowledge argument, *some* physical knowledge and experience has nonetheless been denied to Mary as a result of her confinement. Mary has not been given *all* the physical information after all.

---

[22] As mentioned above, Alter (2013) calls these new increments to Mary's knowledge *phenomenal knowledge$_M$*.

3.2 Color

It turns out the argument about temperature just given can also be used for color, *mutatis mutandis*. Jackson even allowed for this, when he stated "the same style of Knowledge argument could be deployed for taste, hearing, the bodily sensations..." (Jackson 1982, 130) Here is the argument.

Mary is once again in the black and white room. Note that since Mary connects to the outside world through black and white TV and streaming, then she also will see shades of gray. For example, without shading, it would be impossible to convey images of 3D objects (as shading conveys 3D structure), fMRI scans would lack the shading necessary to convey differences in activation levels in the brain, and so forth. But further, shades of gray would in principle be ineliminable, as shadows in her room would appear in shades of gray. Mary then, will be familiar with shades of gray.

It turns out that color scientists consider white, gray and black to be colors. We certainly see white, gray and black in well-lit surroundings. But under these conditions, the rods in our retina are fully saturated, and so are not delivering signals on these shades. However, our cones, which detect the colors, are fully functioning. So it turns out that Mary experiences white, gray and black by means of the exact same detectors that mediate color vision: her cones.

Recall now our previous discussion of temperature. Mary could sense temperatures across a wide range. Despite this, she could not experience some temperatures because a temperature range was enforced in her room. A similar situation is occurring now for Mary with the chromatic colors (red, yellow, green, etc). Externalism regards all the colors, chromatic and achromatic (white, gray, black) to be properties of external objects, for example, reflectances (Dretske 1995, Byrne and Hilbert 2003, Hilbert 1987, Tye 1995, 2000).

Returning once more to temperatures, confinement restricted Mary's experience to a limited range from 98.6 degrees to 500 degrees. Mary then exited the room, exposing her to new physical properties and novel causal interactions between these properties and her sensory systems—including in particular, temperatures of 98.5 degrees and below.

With regard to sensing colors, Mary was previously allowed to experience only a limited reflectance range of white, grays, and black. Mary is now allowed to exit the room, exposing her to new physical properties and novel causal interactions with her sensory systems. These interactions include in particular, new reflectances, which encompass novel chromatic color ranges.

Just as Mary knew a lot about thermodynamics and temperature, Mary knows a great deal about color and its perception. For example, she knows (**K**) about the reflectance for red (**R**). But, she understands, as she did for temperatures, that her *knowledge* (through channels other than immediate experience of red—for example from instruction through her black and white television) of the reflectance for red will be categorically different from any *experience* of that reflectance. That is, $K(R) \neq E(R)$. Analogously to temperatures, there are very good reasons for this: Mary has *already* experienced colors—white, gray, and black. Her experiences of color were delivered by the same sensory system—mediated by her cones—that produces the experience of a color like red. Mary, it turns out, *knows* what it is like to *experience* a color. Therefore she fully expects that a new color experience will be different, as it will involve a novel external property, to wit R, with a new, previously uninstantiated, internal vehicle E.

As was the case for temperature, Mary already understands from her own personal history and research that her knowledge states about external reflectance properties differ in feel from her experiences of external color reflectances. Further, she understands that knowledge of black's reflectance (call this reflectance B) is different from experiencing black. She fully knows why. When Mary ruminates on the reflectance properties for black, she exemplifies a knowledge state $K(B)$, where the state K, she knows, does not occur in visual cortex, but elsewhere in her brain. When experiencing black, Mary has an experience $E(B)$, where the state E, she knows, is a neural state in her visual cortex, and black, B, is a property of an external object. Similarly for white, and shades of gray. Her extensive knowledge of neuroscience informs Mary of those regions activated in *knowledge* of colors (in opposition to the *experience* of) which include left inferior temporal, left posterior parietal, left frontal cortex, and other areas (Martin et al. 1995; D'Esposito et al. 1997; Chao and Martin 1999; Wiggs et al. 1999; Miceli et al. 2001.) Mary also knows that visual cortex is a separate region from these, and is crucially involved in direct experiences of color. (Zeki 1993; Martin et al. 1995; D'Esposito 1997; Wiggs et al. 1999; Miceli et al. 2001; Chao and Martin 1999; Noppeney and Price 2003) Mary understands, as she did with temperatures, that different neural vehicles, involved with different types of contents, will feel different. However, this is to be expected, as distinct physical states will have different physical properties (different neurons in separate brain regions) and will exhibit distinct causal antecedents and effects: immediate covariational causes for E, and historical (from learning) causes for K; glancing at the black pawns when in state $E(B)$, and ruminating about reflectance curves after thinking $K(B)$. Why *would* such disparate states feel similar?

As with her knowledge of temperature, Mary understands that her knowledge states are different in kind from color experiences which are direct, covariational relations with surface reflectance properties. Mary has experienced white, grays, and black, so she knows what it is like to experience colors. Color properties, which have been sensed through visual channels including her cones, have produced her color experiences. Therefore Mary understands that when she exits the room, and has her first experience of red, this experience will be distinct from any knowledge of red. As we saw for temperature, the vehicles **E** and **K** will be altogether different: experience vehicles occurring in visual cortex, and knowledge vehicles occurring in frontal cortex. The causal roles for these two types of state (the antecedents causing these vehicles and the events which follow from them) will also differ: immediate covariational causes for **E**, and historical causes for **K**.

3.3 Thinking about Experience, or Rejecting the Assumption

For an externalist, when Mary exits her room she gains new, physical, knowledge. Externalism denies, then, that Mary has all the physical knowledge *while being confined to her room*. Confining Mary places limits on physical knowledge that she can have. The knowledge argument's claim that Mary can have all the physical information while being confined is mistaken.

An interesting remark on Mary's exit from the room is that she will "realize how impoverished her conception of the mental life of others has been all along." (Jackson 1985, p. 292) But it has just been shown that a brilliant neuroscientist like Mary has already recognized this impoverishment from examination of her own situation, before even exiting the room. And because she recognizes this from her own situation, then *of course* she already realizes it about other people. Mary recognizes that *thinking*—with a neural state **K**—about an external property is not in any way like an immediate *experience* of that property with the senses. Mary's thinking about 190 degrees differs completely from her experiencing 190 degrees, and her thinking about some shade of gray differs completely from an experience of that shade. Mary can simply do measurements on herself regarding properties she is allowed contact with inside the room. Mary can ruminate about 190 degrees, and contrast such a thought with experiencing immersing her pinkie in a freshly poured cup of coffee. Mary knows these will be distinct. Perhaps she studies her lab books and notices she has never experienced temperatures between 175 degrees and 205 degrees. She then contemplates this range of temperatures, thinks carefully about 190 degrees. She realizes that thoughts about 190 degrees are completely different from the direct experience of 190 degrees. She can do an experiment in her room to confirm this. Mary can stick her head in the black and white fMRI device in the room and observe the black and white terminal showing frontal cortex activations when she has thoughts (**K**) about 190 degrees, and then observe activations in her somatosensory cortex when she sticks her finger into the coffee to experience (**E**) 190 degrees. It does not escape her notice that the two states differ altogether in feel, and in addition have distinct physical causes and physical effects. So, just because Mary has not yet experienced 190 degrees at time **t** but then goes on to experience 190 degrees at a later time $t + dt$, it does not follow that she will thereby acquire non-physical knowledge. Instead, what follows is Mary will acquire new *physical* information from the experience—specifically **E**(190 degrees).

3.4 Re-evaluating Mary

By blocking direct access for Mary to some physical properties outside of her room, the knowledge argument effectively denies a portion of the physical world to her. A consequence of this confinement is to deny certain kinds of knowledge—experiential knowledge—of these physical properties.

Recall the two positions on knowledge and experience that were discussed earlier: one position being to deny experience as knowledge, and the other being to accept experience as knowledge. Should experience not be counted a kind of knowledge, Mary nevertheless gains knowledge when stepping out of her room that is parasitic on her experience of a novel physical property: this is the knowledge that Mary experiences Red at $t + dt$, and the knowledge that others have similarly experienced Red as Mary has just done. Since this knowledge requires Mary to experience a physical property that she has heretofore been denied through her confinement, it is new, physical, knowledge at $t + dt$. Tim Crane also recognized this, by saying Mary did not have access to either truth 'not because it is a truth about some mysterious non-physical feature of the world, but because it is the kind of truth that requires the knower to have an experience.'(Crane 2012, 197)

The other option is to count experiences as a kind of knowledge. Under this option, when Mary leaves her room she acquires new physical knowledge: experiential knowledge. In the externalist view, both knowledge and experience are physical relations. An experience will combine an internal experiential vehicle (a neural state), an external physical property (color, temperature, etc) which is experienced, and a direct sensory causal connection between the state and the property. Any such experience, or experiential knowledge, will extend beyond the neural vehicle in the brain, and will include properties and regularities in the world external to the brain.

When we constrain Mary to her room, she is thereby blocked from immediate access to some physical properties in the external world. Such a barrier blocks the physical relations required for any experience of new physical properties outside the room, which will deny some kinds of experiential, physical, knowledge to Mary.

Because experience is extended, such physical barriers will always put limits on Mary's knowledge. Externalism thus says that premise (1) of the knowledge argument, that Mary has all the physical knowledge at time t, is false. And this is because this premise itself relies on the hidden assumption (3) that Mary can have all the physical knowledge while confined in her room. Externalism rejects this assumption because by its very construction it denies crucial physical knowledge to Mary. A different argument than what the knowledge argument has provided is required against a materialist externalist view. Though the knowledge argument has some merit against materialist internalists, it simply misses the mark against an externalist formulation of materialism.

Conclusion

We have now examined three famous arguments against materialism and found that, though each poses a challenge in some way to internalist theories of mind, they all miss the mark against, and indeed do not even apply to, externalist formulations of sensory experience. These three dogmas of internalism—the assumptions that each will apply equally well to all forms of materialism—have been revealed to be mistaken.

The first dogma we considered was Nagel's famous what-it-is-like argument. Here it was shown that he dismissed potential externalist accounts such as functionalism, out of hand, as lacking in subjective properties altogether. Nagel then turned to internalist formulations of materialism, saying that if these theories are true, then the challenge is for them to explain why there is something it is like, *intrinsically,* to undergo them as internal physical processes. Nagel leaves this issue unresolved, and we then considered a different issue with Nagel's account, which was that the notion of what-it-is-like is not in fact a single notion, but rather a collection of three different notions: the what-it-is-likeness of having a mental economy, the what-it-is-likeness of having a subjective point of view, and the what-it-is-likeness of qualia. We then discussed how, with time, it has transpired that the third notion is the one that is now considered to be the "hard" problem of consciousness, and so was the one worth focusing attention on, and indeed, would be the focus of the arguments put forward by Kripke and Jackson. The upshot of the Nagel discussion was that he dismissed the functionalist/externalist accounts of materialism and focused his attention on internalist materialism instead. We will see shortly that externalism does have a reply to these claims by Nagel, but I will first conclude about the Kripke and Jackson arguments before returning to them.

The second dogma we considered was Kripke's modal argument against materialism. This argument was found to only address internalism and ignore externalist accounts. Yet, interestingly, the externalist can use the Kripkean notion of rigid designation for an improved materialist formulation of the causal basis of how sensory systems pick out their properties in the environment. This formulation avoids the extra 'feelings' between internal neural states and the external properties these states have the biological function of indicating. Externalism points out that it is these external physical properties which are 'felt' in our experiences: they are qualia.

The third dogma considered was Jackson's Mary argument. This argument was found to have some force against internalist materialist formulations, but to miss the mark against externalism. We found that constraining Mary to her room had the consequence of blocking her from some physical properties in the world, and this confinement denied some kinds of experiential knowledge to Mary. Because experience is extended in materialist externalism, physical barriers can put limits on Mary's knowledge. As with the Kripkean argument above, the contents of experiences—*qualia*—which are real physical properties in the world, are external to Mary's brain. If these properties are denied to Mary because of her confinement, then there is some experiential (and other forms of) knowledge that will be denied to her until she exits the room.

We are now ready to return to the original Nagel argument that dismissed functionalism as 'neobehaviorist' because, according to Nagel, it failed to deal with the subjective character of mental states. This may be a fairly reasonable accounting of traditional functionalism, in which a mental state is taken to be a relation between inputs, internal mental states, and outputs. Challenges to functionalism like Block's China walkie-talkie argument (Block 1978) and Searle's beer-cans-on-a-string argument (Searle, 1992) seem to back up this characterization by showing that such an instantiation of properties and formal relations leaves out the most important part of experience: qualia. However, externalism can be seen as a kind of functionalism that avoids this charge in a way in which Block and Searle did not consider: the qualia *are* actually accounted for in externalist functionalist accounts of experience. The quale of an experience is the content of the experience: the external property which is sensed, and which causes the internal experiential state; the latter of which has the biological function of indicating that type of property in the environment. This is shown in the externalist formulations of the experiences of pain, temperature, color, and so on, which have been demonstrated in this paper through the replies to Kripke and Jackson. So qualia have been there all along and in plain view for externalist functional accounts. And these accounts not only avoid many problems which crop up for internalism—Nagel's purported lack of an 'intrinsic' what-it-is-like property; Kripke's 'felt pain' which was somehow supposed to be picked out by a qualitative 'sensation' inserted between the pain and a neural state; and Jackson's nonphysical information or knowledge—they *explain* them. Externalism gives a materialist account of qualia and experience that avoids these problems in a way that satisfies biological, neuroscientific, and physical naturalism. This account also dispels the three dogmas of internalism.

Personal note on Fred Dretske

An anecdote from Paul Skokowski:

I first met Fred Dretske in January 1988, when I was a third-year Ph.D. student at Stanford. I had just finished reading *Knowledge and the Flow of Information*, and was especially excited about the analog/digital distinction for information content. I went in to talk with my advisor John Perry about the book, when he told me that it just so happened that Fred was currently visiting Stanford as a Fellow at the Center for Advanced Study in the Behavioral Sciences. When I asked if he thought Fred might be willing to meet me, John didn't hesitate to pick up the phone, call the Center, and get Fred on the line. We set up a meeting for the following week.

Fred and I hit it off immediately. The reason, I am convinced, is that he had originally studied electrical engineering, and I, physics, and we shared both a common technical language, and a mutual desire to explain mental phenomena in physical terms, or as Fred put it in *Knowledge and the Flow of Information*, to "…bake a mental cake out of physical yeast and flour." (p. xi) Fred was finishing his book *Explaining Behavior* during his time at the Center, and he started feeding me the draft chapters. I would meet with him every other week and discuss details of the chapters, and to have what to me were novel and exciting discussions on information, representation, mental content, and causation in general.

Fred came to Stanford at a fortunate time for my graduate studies. I was doing the Ph.D. part time on a scholarship while working full time as a research physicist at the Lawrence Livermore National Lab. John Perry's brilliance here was to recognize that Fred was the right fit for my philosophical interests and background and to make a connection between us.

The conversations with Fred were terrific and set me on a new path of thinking about the mind. Fred and I discussed how neural networks could serve as a physical vehicle for the executive states that carried content and caused behavior in the ways Fred was developing in *Explaining Behavior*. Fred encouraged me to flesh out these intuitions with further research into neural networks and other fields including neuroscience to find neural mechanisms that worked in the right ways. I was lucky to be able to take classes on the foundations of neural networks from David Rumelhart, who had also just arrived at Stanford, and who later served on my committee. This background research set the groundwork for my dissertation.

I continued working with Fred and John for the next year and a half, and beginning in November 1990 the University of California granted me a year's sabbatical. This was perfect timing because Fred was just starting his appointment at The Farm. Fred became my primary advisor, and in this way I became Fred's first Ph.D. student at Stanford. One day I went to see John Perry—before Fred Dretske—because I found what appeared to be a flaw in Fred's causal story in *Explaining Behavior*. But I also realized it could be fixed, and in a completely Dretskean style. As I scribbled the notations on the board, John Perry sat back and said, "Paul, I think you've got your dissertation topic." I said that was wonderful, but how could I tell Fred about a problem with his own theory? "Leave that to me," he said. A few days later I went to see Fred, and I still see him sitting at his desk, smiling, saying "John tells me you think you've got a dissertation idea. Show it to me." I did, and Fred very graciously agreed that it would work. I soon began writing, and when I'd finished the first chapter, Fred had me send it out for my first philosophy publication. Fred read every word I wrote carefully, gave great advice, and as a result, the dissertation was finished within that sabbatical year.

Fred continued to be a mentor and colleague to me in subsequent years. I occasionally saw him after he retired and moved to North Carolina in 1998, most often at APA conferences. In 2011 I saw we were both presenting at the San Diego APA, and we met for dinner and martinis. Over dinner I thanked Fred for everything he had done to help me as a philosopher, including, especially, inspiring me to finish my Ph.D. in philosophy. I only saw Fred one more time, at the Seattle APA the following year. Though I never got the chance to talk to him again after that, I am honored to have had him as my advisor at Stanford, as a philosophical colleague, and as a friend.

References

Alter, T. 2013. Social Externalism and the Knowledge Argument. *Mind,* 122(486):481-496.

Ball, D. 2009. There are no phenomenal concepts. *Mind,* 118(472):935-962.

Block, N. 1978. Troubles with Functionalism, *Minnesota Studies in the Philosophy of Science,* 9:261-325.

Byrne, A., and Hilbert, D. 2003. Color Realism and Color Science. *Behavioral and Brain Sciences,* 26:3-21.

Chao, L., and Martin, A. 1999. Cortical regions associated with perceiving, naming, and knowing about colors. *Journal of Cognitive Neuroscience,* 11(1): 25-35.

Crane, T. 2012. Tye on Acquaintance and the Problem of Consciousness. *Philosophy and Phenomenological Research,* 84(1): 190-198.

D'Esposito, M. et al. 1996. A functional MRI study of mental image generation. *Neuropsychologia,* 35(5): 725-730.

Dretske, F. 1981. *Knowledge and the Flow of Information.* Cambridge, MA: Bradford/MIT Press.

Dretske, F. 1988. *Explaining Behavior*. Cambridge, MA: MIT Press.

Dretske, F.1990. Seeing, Believing, and Knowing. *An Invitation to Cognitive Science*, ed. D. Osherson, 129-148. Cambridge: MIT Press.

Dretske, F. 1995. *Naturalizing the Mind*. Cambridge, MA: MIT Press.

Gazzaniga, M., Ivry, R., and Mangun, G. 2002. *Cognitive Neuroscience: The Biology of the Mind*, New York, NY: W.W. Norton and Company.

Goldman, D. 1970. *A Theory of Human Action*. Prentice Hall.

Hilbert, D. 1987. *Color and Color Perception: A Study in Anthropocentric Realism*. Stanford: Center for the Study of Language and Information Press.

Horgan, T. 1984. Jackson on Physical Information and Qualia. *Philosophical Quarterly,* 34:147-152.

Jackson, F. 1982. Epiphenomenal Qualia. *Philosophical Quarterly*, 32:127-136.

Jackson, F. 1985). What Mary Didn't Know. *Journal of Philosophy*, 83:291-295.

Jackson, F. 2003. Mind and Illusion. *Minds and Persons*, ed. Anthony O'Hear, 251-271. Royal Institute of Philosophy, Supplement 53, Cambridge: Cambridge University Press.

Jackson, F. 2006. Consciousness. *Handbook of Philosophy*, ed. Frank Jackson and Michael Smith. Oxford University Press.

Kim, J. 1973. Causation, Nomic Subsumption, and the Concept of Event. *Journal of Philosophy*, 70(8):217-236.

Kripke, S. 1980. *Naming and Necessity*. Cambridge, MA: Harvard University Press.

Kuhn, T. 1962. *The Structure of Scientific Revolutions*. Chicago: University of Chicago Press.

Mackie, J.L. 1974. *The Cement of the Universe: A Study of Causation*. Oxford University Press.

Martin, A., et al. 1995. Discrete cortical regions associated with knowledge of color and knowledge of action. *Science*, 270:102-105.

Miceli, G., et al. 2001. The dissociation of color from form and function knowledge. *Nature Neuroscience*, 4(6): 662-667.

Nagel, T. 1974. What is it like to be a bat?. *Philosophical Review*, 83: 435-50.

Noppeney, U., and Price, C. 2003. Functional imaging of the semantic system: Retrieval of sensory-experienced and verbally learned knowledge. *Brain and Language*, 84(1): 120-133.

Perry, J. 2001. *Knowledge, Possibility, and Consciousness*. Cambridge, MA: MIT Press.

Place, U.T. 1956. Is Consciousness a Brain Process? *British Journal of Psychology*, 47: 44-50.

Purves, D., et al. 2001. *Neuroscience*. Sunderland, MA: Sinauer Associates.

Putnam, H. 1968. Brains and Behaviour. *Analytical Philosophy: Second Series*, ed. R.J. Butler, 1-19. Oxford: Blackwell.

Quine, W.V.O. and Ullian, J.S. 1970. *The Web of Belief*. New York: Random House.

Searle, J. 1992. *The Rediscovery of the Mind*. MIT Press, Cambridge, MA.

Skokowski, P. 2002. I, Zombie. *Consciousness and Cognition,* 11:1-9.

Skokowski, P. 2003. The Right Kind of Content for a Physicalist About Color." *Behavioral and Brain Sciences,* 26: 790-790.

Skokowski, P. 2004. Structural Content: A Naturalistic Approach to Implicit Belief. *Philosophy of Science*, 71(3).

Skokowski, P. 2007. Is the Pain in Jane Felt Mainly in Her Brain?" *Harvard Review of Philosophy*, 15: 58-71.

Smart, J.J.C. 1959. Sensations and Brain Processes. *Philosophical Review*, 68:141-156.

Stoljar, D. 2001. Two Conceptions of the Physical. *Philosophy and Phenomenological Research*, 62:253-270.

Tolman, R. 1956. *Principles of Statistical Mechanics*. Oxford: Oxford University Press.

Tye, M. 1995. *Ten Problems of Consciousness*. Cambridge, MA: MIT Press.

Tye, M. 2000. *Consciousness, Color, and Content*. Cambridge, MA: MIT Press.

Tye, M. 2009. *Consciousness Revisited*. Cambridge, MA: MIT Press.

Wiggs, C., Weisberg, J. and Martin, A. 1999. Neural Correlates of semantic and episodic memory retrieval. *Neuropsychologia*, 37:103-118.

Zeki, S. 1993. *A Vision of the Brain*. Oxford: Blackwell Scientific Publications.

5

Perceptual Activity and the Object of Perception: Which of the Many Things That Are Causes of a Sensory Impression is the One That is Being Perceived?

DENNIS STAMPE

Introduction

The Causal Theory of Perception contends that what we perceive—the thing we see, hear, taste, feel or smell—is the thing that *causes* the visual, auditory, gustatory, tactile or olfactory sensation or impression in our minds. So we see this table: while there are many tables, even in this room, that look exactly like this one, the only table we are *seeing* is the one that is now causing something to look to us like a table, *i.e.* causing a tabloid visual impression in each of our minds. We are not seeing those tables that are *not* causing that impression, though they may be otherwise exactly like this one. But something more is required to be seeing this table, for there are many things in addition to this table that are causing that tabloid impression, and we are not seeing all of those things. The question was vividly put by Henry Price back in 1932:

Information and Mind: The Philosophy of Fred Dretske.
Paul Skokowski (ed.).
Copyright © 2020, CSLI Publications.

> [I]t cannot be said that the table is *the* cause of the sense-data .... On the one hand, why should we go so far back? Why not say that the light rays are the cause of the sense-datum—or the retina, or the brain. All these have as good a right to be called 'the' [unique] cause of it as the table has—that is, neither they nor the table has any right at all. But on the other hand, why not go farther back still? Why stop at the table? The electric light, the wires conveying the current, the dynamo which generates it—all these are just as necessary to the genesis of the sense-datum as the table itself is. (Price 1965, p. 397)

So here is our question: which of the many things that are causes of a sensory impression is the one that is being perceived? Or, more accurately, which causes are among the specific few that are being perceived? For there are generally more than one: we hear both the sound of the train and (therefore) the train, but not the engineer driving the train, nor our eardrums vibrating from the sound of it, though each of these items is equally a cause of our auditory impression.[1]

1   Methodological Preliminaries

One might attempt to answer the question by identifying the particular way in which the object perceived causes the percept, the particular causal process connecting just that object to the impression—in the case of sight, the reflection or emission of light from that object, the light stimulating the light-sensitive cells in the retina of the eye. This is not the way the dynamo causes the percept, nor the way the neural activity in the retina causes it; the process by which these links in the causal chain make their specific contribution is not by the transmission of light. But this is still too rough, for if we are seeing the table by daylight, the sun also causes the percept of the table and it *does* do so by the transmission of light. Nevertheless, we are not seeing the sun. That can perhaps be fixed by a finer specification of the relevant process. So, similarly for the other sensory modalities, one by one, we may identify the distinctive mechanism by which the object *e.g. felt* causes a tactile impression, which will differ from the way other factors in the causal process cause that impression.

Such an answer to our question, however, is unacceptable on the traditional conception of philosophical analysis. For on that conception an analysis of a concept does something more than identify the conditions under

---

[1] I chose to read this paper at Stanford's symposium commemorating Fred Dretske, who was my colleague at Madison for nearly thirty years, because it was the first philosophical topic that he and I ever discussed, back in 1966, and the last, in 2013. A draft of this paper was the last piece of mine that he read. His comments were helpful, as always. I would also thank Alan Sidelle, Elliott Sober, Kevin Possin, Martha Gibson and Jennifer Stampe for helpful discussion.

which something falls under that concept. An analysis provides, in addition, a representation of the conceptual abilities and the knowledge that anyone in possession of that concept employs in applying it to instances, and in drawing inferences from propositions involving that concept. So the terms in which the analysis is stated must express just concepts and knowledge that the competent user of the concept under analysis possesses, and *must* possess, to *be* in possession of that concept. And a person can certainly have the concept of seeing something without knowing the first thing about the transmission of light.

This was the reason Dretske gave in *Seeing and Knowing* for rejecting the Causal Theory. (Dretske 1969) He was assuming, evidently, that the *only* way the relevant cause could be singled out by the causal theorist was by identifying the distinctive causal process by which the perceived object caused the percept. So the Causal Theory, he said, would entail that *before* the discovery of the transmission of light no one even knew the meaning of the verb 'to see.'[2]

It is reported, as you may have heard, that half of college students believe that the eyes see by shooting rays out to the object seen—rather like Superman's X-ray vision, though ordinary eye-rays are not so penetrating. (See Winer et al. 2002) Even so, these students do know what the word 'see' means, and they do possess the concept it expresses.

So a completion of the Causal Theory that drags in 'expert knowledge' of the causal processes of perception makes the analysis *too rich* to be a correct analysis on the classical model. Paul Grice, recognizing this, proposed a clever way to get around this problem.[3] The analysis might specify the relevant cause not by an over-informative description of it, but merely by simple *ostension*. One might say that the thing seen must cause the visual percept in the same kind of way that some demonstrated paradigm object—a red 'pillar box,' as Grice had it—seen in broad daylight, causes the visual impression; or let it be the way that this table right here is presently causing our tabloid perceptions. That suffices to identify the specific 'kind of way' an impression is caused by an object when the object is therefore seen. The further, more informative, identification of that 'kind of way' —as mediated by the transmission of light, *etc.*—might be discoverable by the scientist, and known to only those who know the science, but no such further knowledge is required for one to have the concept of seeing an object and the ability to use it with such success as such possession requires. One may even harbor a 'fundamental misunderstanding' of the nature of that process. Our ill-

---

[2] This was also assuming that the correct analysis of a concept explains our knowledge of the meaning of the term expressing that concept.

[3] "The Causal Theory of Perception", reprinted in Swartz. *op. cit.*

informed students may have successfully acquired the concept from some such paradigm, even if they got the rest of their conception of seeing from Superman comics.

But just as an analysis can be too fat, larded with too much extra-conceptual information, so it may be too *lean*. And Grice's analysis might be faulted on that score. It would be *too lean* if it were impossible for us to extract from the analysis — as corollaries, if you will — such truths as that seeing ordinarily involves the use of the eyes, or that the closer you get the better you see or hear, or that you cannot feel things that are out of your reach, or that you cannot taste a thing without bits of it touching your tongue.[4] We non-experts know more, *a priori*, about the nature of the relevant causal connection than Grice's suggestion, unamplified, would imply.

In *Knowledge and the Flow of Information* (1981), Dretske came back to the problem, rejecting the Causal Theory again, but this time for its inadequacy to solve the problem under discussion. He denied "that a causal analysis can give a satisfactory account of the object of our sensory experience. It provides no way of discriminating among the variety of eligible candidates" (Dretske 1981, p. 157). He offered a new solution[5] that turned not on the specific way what we perceive causes a sensory impression, but instead on "the way in which informational relationships operate to determine what it is that we perceive."

Dretske's idea was that the object perceived is one about which the percept might *carry information*. This is plausible *a priori*, for it does seem to be part of our concept of 'a thing perceived' that it is a thing of which we might attain some knowledge *from* our sensory impression of it. That is to

---

[4] You can feel something that is out of hand's reach with a stick, if you can reach it with a stick; but if you can reach something, even if only with a stick, it's not entirely out of reach.

[5] What had been his solution in *Seeing and Knowing*? Of course only a *causal* theorist, which Dretske was not, is faced with the particular question, Which of the *causes* of the impression is the object one sees? But anyone faces the more general question, Which of the many *things* crucially involved (in whatever way) in the perceptual event is the object that one sees? In *Seeing and Knowing* (Chicago, 1969) it was held, plausibly, to be necessary that the object seen should *look some or way or other* to the seer. And, we may note, such unperceived causes as the retinal image, or the dynamo, do *not* look some way to the perceiver. So might this provide an answer to our general question? (I would argue that it is a covertly *circular* account. See "a *quale*-tative' answer" in the appendix below.) This line is available also to the causal theorist, though adopting it compromises the purity of the resulting causal theory, for a thing's looking some way is not a *causal* factor that identifies the object seen. One might try saying that the thing being seen is that *cause* (of the visual image) that looks some way to the seer. But the fact that the object *causes* the visual image would then do no work in the analysis. Or: either the crucial concept— of a thing's looking some way to someone—is left unanalyzed, which is unsatisfactory, or else analyzed as requiring such a thing to *cause* it to look to the seer as if something or other were the case. And then our question resurfaces. The line to be explored in the present paper may avoid this particular complaint.

say, on Dretske's view of knowledge, that it is part of our concept that the character of those impressions (thus the way it therein looks, or feels, *etc.*, to us) might contain some *information* about the thing we see or feel. This is so even given Dretske's definition of information: that is, the occurrence of the impression (thus, something's looking F) might rule out any possibility of the thing's *not* being F, if conditions are such as to preclude that possibility, as they may be.

So far, so good. This much—this *necessary* condition for being a perceived object—could be wrung out of the concept under analysis without *a posteriori* supplementation. It would seem to rule out the more distant causes—Price's dynamo, or the table-maker— for the impression carries no genuine information about them. But what about the states of the perceptual process nearer us on the causal chain from the perceived object, like the state of the retina? One might have thought that our impressions contain information about such more proximal states too, as well as the object intuitively perceived. (We needn't be able to *access* such information, of course, for it to *be* there.)

But that thought—according to *Knowledge and the Flow*[6]—would be false. The fact is that the impression *does not* carry information about those more proximal causes of the percept. It does not carry information about such causes as the retinal states, or their relevant properties, because even given the occurrence of the resulting percept, the conditional probability of any particular intermediary state having the properties it has is something less than one. According to Dretske, this is a fact bound up with perceptual *constancy*—the relatively constant appearance the objects of perception present, compared with the variable character of the intermediary states and the variety of neural pathways through which information flows. As we travel from percept out and down the causal chain, we as it were *see through* those links about which the percept contains no information until we arrive at the first link about which we *do* receive genuine information. And *that* is the object perceived.

Dretske's account is based upon facts about perception of undoubted importance. But whatever its merits by other measures, the analysis is *too rich* to be right, if measured by the standards of classical conceptual analysis. (Those were the standards to which the Causal Theory was held in Dretske's first book, but in his second, those standards have been abandoned.) For just as someone who has the full concept of seeing something may be ignorant of the transmission of light, surely one may be ignorant of relative probabilities conferred upon the various states in the causal chain by the occurrence of the

---

[6] Chapter 6, especially pff. 155; especially pp. 162-164. There is far more to Dretske's treatment of this problem than is reflected in this too cursory review of it.

visual percept. One may have not the slightest conception of such stuff. One may not know that there is information contained in the percept *only* about the thing intuitively perceived.

I make no criticism of Fred on this score. Maybe the old standard of conceptual analysis must be abandoned. Certainly it *may* be abandoned for some purposes, and genuinely philosophical purposes too. Indeed Fred spoke now about "the informational basis of these distinctions," not about an *analysis* of the concept of the object perceived. The differences between objects and other causes may very well *have* an "informational basis" even if that is not the basis upon which we ordinarily make the distinctions. There may yet be some informational factors that implicitly shape the concepts we employ. But even if this is so, it is hard to think that we cannot do more toward clarifying the notion of the thing seen or heard or felt—the object perceived—in terms of simpler concepts that are in everyone's explicit command.

In short, Dretske's claim is that "the causal theory has no way of discriminating among viable candidates for the role of thing perceived." This claim was too hasty. For there is one viable candidate whose file was never opened. I think it deserves at least one interview.

2   Perceptual Activity and the Object Perceived

A factor that has been strangely ignored in this discussion is the *perceptual activity performed by the perceiver*: the perceiver's act of feeling, smelling, tasting, of looking at or listening to some one (or rather a certain few) of the many things that form links in the causal chain that results, step by step, in the eventual percept, and traces back down into the past and out of our ken. By a perceptual activity I mean a bit of a perceiver's *behavior*—such physical activities as reaching out and touching a thing with the fingertips, inhaling the air in which a thing is located, putting the thing in one's mouth and chewing it up, turning one's eyes toward it and scanning it, turning one's ears toward it and approaching it more closely. These are acts done to some particular thing or things and not others involved in the perceptual process: the thing is sniffed, felt, chewed, swallowed. Or they are acts of looking or listening or smelling that open us up to, or make us physically subject, to the causal influence of the things to which those acts are directed. The verbs 'feel', 'smell', and 'taste' name the perceptual activity or behavior in question. The verbs 'see' and 'hear' do not do so. There are imperatives with the former three verbs ('Taste this.' *etc*.) but no similar imperative 'See this!', or "Hear this!' (except in the U.S. Navy? And once we had 'Hark!'.). Instead we say 'Look at this' or 'Listen to this'.

The suggestion I wish to try out is that *it is the thing to which (etc.) a relevant perceptual activity is thus done or directed, that is the thing being perceived*. The idea is almost stupidly simple. Which one of the many causes of our visual impressions of this table is the one that we are *seeing*? How about this? It's the one we are *looking* at. We are looking at *this* table, not the one in the back of the room, nor are we looking at the maker of the table or looking inside our skulls at our brains. And this thing we are looking at is the thing we are seeing, the thing that is *relevantly* causing our tabloid impression. Looking at things is, of course, a kind of perceptual activity or behavior,[7] and one's looking at a thing is a *cause* of one's having a visual percept or impression—indeed an impression *of* the very thing *at* which one is looking. The cells in your retina or their activities are another cause of that visual impression, but you are not looking at those things, and you are not seeing them. Nor are you looking at the dynamo generating the electricity making the light, and just as you are not *looking at* those things you are not *seeing* them either, though they are causes of your visual impression.

It should be acknowledged immediately that there are internal senses that involve no apparent perceptual activity: the perception of bodily disturbances and conditions, heartburn and hunger, various forms of proprioception, and so on. There is nothing for us to do to perceive our orientation in space—our being, for instance, currently right side up. The force of gravity and those blobs (*cupulae*) inside the semicircular canals do it all for us. The suggestion to be explored is not that *all* things perceived are objects of perceptual action. It is not likely that the concept of perceptual object is governed throughout its wide range of application by any single factor. But I propose to explore this one factor where it does play a role, and the relation between the two concepts, that is, between the object of perceptual activity and of the object perceived, as well as the nature of that relationship, and the range of perceptual phenomena in which the concepts coincide.

These include particularly the external senses, especially those that involve immediate contact with the object perceived. The paradigm case is feeling. And yes of course even here, you can perceptually feel things without performing any act of feeling or touching: the things you feel may touch *you*, like the bug crawling up your leg. But even here the thing you are feeling is doing something essentially like what you yourself do when you actively feel a thing—it is pressing something against your skin— doing something that causes an object to cause a tactile sensation. The factor under discussion, then, is perceptual action or *what happens in perceptual action* or as a result

---

[7] Looking and listening and smelling are things we do, but, to be accurate, not things we *do to* the things looked at or listened to or smelled, as feeling and tasting a thing *is* doing something *to* it. The general concept required is that of a perceptual action, and of the object designated by the grammatical object of the verb predicating that action of an agent. The hypothesis is that the object designated by that expression is the thing perceived.

of one, whoever or whatever the agent may be, and even if in particular cases the *perceiver* doesn't perform that action or do anything to make that thing happen.

So let's consider, point by point, how the idea works in the case of feeling, how it abides by the rules of classical analysis, and whether it avoids circularity.

I am now feeling this cup: that is, am performing the physical act of my running my fingertips over it.

(1) This physical act, this event, again and obviously, *is a cause* of the tactile sensation; it explains why the cup causes the sensation, which it would not do but for my running my fingertips over it. So, as one may say, it is the cause of the cup's *causing* the sensation.

(2) It is not the *activity of feeling* the cup that is the object of the tactile perception—that object is the cup. I do not feel the *activity*—I do not tactilely feel it, that is. (I do not tactilely feel myself feeling the cup or feel my feeling of the cup, though I may *kinesthetically* do so, in part, as I feel the movements of my arm and fingers feeling the cup.) The *object* of the tactile perception is the thing that is *touched*, not the touching of it.

(3) This proposal excludes the other causes in the causal chain that extends back to the maker of the cup, and thereafter to the coffee shop worker who delivered the cup to my hand. (To exclude such causes—to discriminate them from the object perceived—was the challenge that allegedly the Causal Theory hadn't the resources to meet.) They are excluded by the fact that I am not actively feeling—touching—the maker of the cup or the person who put the cup my hand. More precisely, even if it were the case, bizarrely, that I *am* now feeling those persons, they are excluded because my feeling them is not what is causing these cuppish sensations.[8] My suggestion would exclude, moreover, things and events further up the causal chain that are affected by my physically touching the cup. For neither am I physically touching the nerves under the skin of my fingertips nor the nerves that run up my arm or the cells in my brain the activity of which results in this sensation. Or more precisely, it is not my touching such interior items that would be causing them to cause *these* sensations if, again bizarrely, I should happen to be doing so, perhaps with my left hand. The proposal is that what I am actively feeling, *i.e.* touching, and nothing else, is the thing I am perceptually feeling, provided my touching that thing is what causes it to cause the sensation. I am feeling the very surface of the cup, and also the wall of the cup, though not the inside surface of that wall. That is, I am perceptually feeling exactly those things,

---

[8] If I were touching those persons (as well as the cup) and it was not the cup but *they* who are (yet more strangely) causing these cuppish sensations, then they would be what I am perceptually feeling –*mis*perceiving, pretty badly, but still perceiving.

and only those things, that I am actively feeling, *i.e.*, touching. *We feel just what we feel.*

That statement has the air of a tautology, but the tautological ring of it is owing to a pun. The first 'feel' refers to experiencing a tactile sensation, a conscious state, and the second 'feel' refers to the physical act of touching a thing, running one's fingers over it or the like. I will distinguish these 'feel's with the adverbs 'perceptually' for the first and 'actively' for the second. We *perceptually* feel what we *actively* feel. The verbs 'feel', 'taste', and 'smell' are all homonymous in this way, designating both an action and the normal perceptual result of that action. There is an act of tasting which involves chewing and the things to which this action is done—the food that gets chewed—is what is perceptually tasted. Not the tongue, *etc.*, *etc.*

One can be tripped up by these homonyms. Offended by the odor of the unwashed Dr. Johnson, the lady sharing his coach exclaimed, "Sir! You *smell!"* to which the grammarian, unperturbed, replied, "Madame, *you* smell. I stink." Though Dr. Johnson may disapprove, one *can* say that a thing smells, meaning stinks, as even he might say the coffee smells good. This is part of a pattern in English: what we taste tastes (= has a taste); what we feel feels (= has a feel, perhaps a satiny one); and what we smell smells (= has a smell or aroma). So, just for completeness, this is a third way in which perceptual verbs occur, an intransitive one, that takes the thing perceived as its subject and describes the perceptible quality it presents. This intransitive occurrence of a perceptual verb I will call 'presentational.' The presentational verb is morphologically identical to the verb in its activity or perceptual sense, in the case of 'smell', 'feel' and 'taste'.' There is no presentational form of 'hear' or 'see' (unless 'presents a sight' or 'shows [itself]' are counted).[9] But there are syntactic and semantic analogues: the thing we hear 'sounds' a certain way, and the thing we see 'looks' a certain way.

One last grammatical note. Perceptual verbs in their activity sense might be classified as *causatives*. (Paradigm causatives in English include 'lay'= cause to lie, and 'set' = cause to sit, the transitive verb morphologically kin to the intransitive. *Cf.* 'show'= cause [someone] to see.) To actively taste, smell, or feel something is to cause that thing to (presentationally) taste,

---

[9] One would guess that the presentational form of the verb just *is* the intransitive form of the causative verb, e.g. A's f*eeling* x being A's causing x to f*eel* some way to S. This would imply that if the perceptual verb is *not* grammatically a causative, then there will be no perceptual form of that verb. This is borne out in the fact that there is no presentational form of 'see' and 'hear', just as neither verb is grammatically a causative.

smell, or feel some way *to* the agent of the act.[10] To look at or listen to something is to cause it to look or sound some way (to oneself).

I am feeling the cup. *This* particular act of feeling, of touching, is a *deliberate* act, one which I intend to be doing. But the intention is not essential. We are all of us now feeling the floor beneath our feet, though we had not been intending to feel it. We are feeling all the things that our feet are touching, our socks, the soles of our shoes, and the floor. But not the subfloor. Why not? I don't know. There is a good subsidiary question, here, of 'how deep' a perception goes into the thing perceived, and why just so deep and no deeper. Regarding this question, I say only this: the things perceptually felt go exactly as deep as the act of feeling. If you can't touch it you can't perceptually feel it, because, if you can't touch it you can't feel it in the activity sense. But of course you can touch more than surfaces. Descartes was wrong to say that out the window he saw "no more than hats and coats," not "men themselves."[11]

Of course that involves a confusion of what Dretske called 'epistemic' seeing (seeing *that* it is men wearing those hats and coats, not automata) with 'non-epistemic' or simple seeing (which does not require knowing *what* you are seeing or even having the concept of a man). We are discussing simple perception throughout this essay.[12] The correlative perceptual actions are correspondingly simple in the same sense: the person (or animal) doing the touching, chewing, looking or whatever need have no idea *what* he is touching *etc.* or *that* he is touching anything, or that whatever he is touching is what he is (perceptually) feeling.[13]

I was saying, also, that the concept of the perceptual act does not involve the concept of the perceptual object *via* an intention with which it is necessarily done, *e.g.* the intention to perceive that object. If it did the line of analysis under discussion would be circular. No such intention is necessary. But perhaps the concept of the thing actively perceived is in some more subtle way dependent on the concept of that thing *as* the object of the resulting sensation. If so, there is a problem.

---

[10] The converse is not unambiguously the case: you can cause something to taste a certain way by adding a squeeze of lemon to it, or to look red to you by painting it red –as you can cause a dog to lie at your feet without laying it there.

[11] Second Meditation. He meant that he did not *see that* but rather *judged* that they were men. It does not follow that *what he saw* were not men, of course. The fact is that what he saw were men but he couldn't tell just from what he saw that they were men.

[12] *Cf.* Warnock, "Seeing", reprinted in Swartz; and, for Dretske, Chapter II of *Seeing and Knowing*; and a late defense, his "Perception and Cognition; The Goldilocks Test," in *The Cognitive Penetrability of Perception,* eds. J. Zeimbekis and A. Raftopoulos (Oxford, 2015).

[13] There are further remarks on this topic in an appendix.

We are trying to analyze the concept of the object of perception and must not do so in terms of a second concept that employs the very concept under analysis. That would be going in a circle. It is important, then, that the perceptual activity *not* be thought of as *an attempt* to render something an object of perception, an *attempt e.g.* to feel or see something. For making such an attempt would presuppose a use, on the part of the perceiver, of the *concept* of an object of perception, and our analysis would fail to explain *what* concept that is. So for the purposes of the analysis, the action of feeling a thing must be understood as if it were a merely physical act, *e.g.* of touching, or being touched by, or one physical body being run across the surface of another. The act of smelling is to be understood as the physical act of inhaling air through the nose, and tasting as physical activities in the mouth of biting into and chewing and swallowing.

It is necessary to say this because the statement that the activity was done may seem to *imply* that the cognate perception was forthcoming.[14] So while 'She touched the cup, but couldn't feel it' is acceptable, 'She felt the cup but couldn't feel it' is doubtful: it sounds inconsistent, even if we are clear that the sense of 'feel' in each clause differs. 'She sniffed the stuff but couldn't smell it' is fine, but perhaps not 'she smelled the stuff but couldn't smell it.' The act of 'smelling', so called, seems to require successfully eliciting a smell. Could the person without tactile sensation *feel* the cup—or just *try* to feel it? Can a blind person look at a cat, or merely turn his eyes toward it? (Must the cat look some way or other to one who genuinely looks at it? That seems too strong: what if the cat has gone transparent, like the invisible man? You could still look at it, couldn't you? 'I was looking straight at it, but it had gone transparent.' But maybe if you were completely blind you *couldn't* look at it.)

To analyze the concept of the object perceived we must find a way to identify that object without relying on the fact that it is the object perceived. We are trying to do so in terms of the perceptual action and *its* object, identified in ways that do not illegitimately *presuppose* that it is the object perceived. But if a perceptual acting, *e.g.* of feeling, requires that the object felt should presentationally feel some way to the agent, and if presentational properties are attributable only to the thing perceived, then it seems we are going in a circle.

But it's not necessarily so. The presentational property is attributable to the object *actively* perceived, the thing that we feel in and by *touching* it, and so long as that object is conceived simply in terms of that *physical* component

---

[14] Thanks to Alan Sidelle here.

of the act of feeling, we avoid the circle.[15] The perceptual action breaks down into the physical action of touching and its psychological result, an impression or sensation. This sensation may be conceived in terms of a presentational property belonging to an object perceived, *e.g.,* of feeling a certain way to us, and the meaning of the active form of the perceptual verb does seem to involve this conception. But in the analysis we are trying, the sensation is to be identified simply *as* an event of consciousness with a certain quality that occurs as a causal consequence of a certain physical act of the perceiver. Of course if the analysis succeeds, the *claim* will be that this *is* the object perceived. But this will not have been smuggled in by the backdoor.

Various factors determine the extent to which an animal must perform some perceptual act in order to perceive a given thing (or the extent to which one may be completely passive). These include the nature of the thing itself: you don't need to be listening to hear the thunder crashing, or looking to see a bright flash of lightning. They include also environmental and anatomical factors. Human beings have immobile ears (relative to their heads) and so we do less to hear a thing, and less to improve our hearing of it, than, say, horses, who prick up their ears and turn them to the sound. More accurately, that sensory organ or appendage itself is not in our immediate voluntary control, as are the eyeballs or the fingers or the head on which the ears are fixed. So we do try to hear better by turning our heads, or getting our ears closer to the source of the sound. W*hat* we get closer to is the thing we hear *better*, as a result of our doing so. We, and horses too, do far less to produce auditory perceptions than bats do, who go so far as to make vocal noises and listen to the sound that bounces back to them from things in their vicinity: *what* they hear, then, *are* these echoes, and they thereby perceive—and even, perhaps, 'hear'—the things that send back the echoes.[16] The objects of these auditory perceptions, then, are identified by the perceptual activities that cause them.

---

[15] A similar remark may be made regarding the use, in this analysis, of the expressions 'looking *for*' or 'listening *for*' in describing perceptual activities. It may seem best to make do with just 'looking at' (and plain 'listening') because looking *for* the cat involves the concept of trying to see (visually locate) the cat, and thus the employment, by the searcher, of the concept of the cat as a potential object of perception. But looking for something also involves such physical activities as scanning, looking into place after place, approaching closer, and these aspects of looking for a thing, and their causing the relevant sensation. These may be referred to in the analysis, legitimately, if we abstract away from the intention behind them, and if we do, we will have a truer conception of all that may go into a perceptual activity.

[16] Dretske pointed out that we don't say we 'hear' the sound of the canyon walls when we hear our voice echo from them. Maybe 'hearing x' requires hearing a sound (made or reflected by x) that carries more information about x than that echo does about the canyon. The echoes that guide a bat reportedly carry information about the both the trajectory and the size of the bat's prey.

(The bat, already put to hard use by philosophers, might be the poster animal for the cause I am supporting.)

3   Why has the Role of Perceptual Activity been Ignored?

In all this we are 'assembling reminders' of things we know perfectly well. But our use of the language of perception must be governed by things that we know perfectly well (or at least that all of us believe), and our common command of the concepts the language expresses can involve nothing more. So it is, I think, rather remarkable that the suggestion being explored here, that the object perceived is the object of a perceptual action, has not been even considered. Why has it not?   That we see what we look at is no discovery, or that looking at a thing enables us—causes us to be able—to see it. It *was* a discovery when Copernicus realized that our own movements (we being riders on a moving Earth) explained the apparent movements of the planets; for our movement, *that* perceptual activity, was then unknown. But the movement of our fingertips when we feel an object is perfectly well known, and yet we have not considered that *that* might be the cause of the tactile sensation that determines *what* is being felt. Our own activity is invisible to us when we look at a thing and see it—invisible to us philosophically as well. It is worth asking why this might be so.

One reason is that we put the question in a way that blinds us to this factor. In effect we put the question to ourselves in this form:

Q "Which of the many causes of our perceptual impression is *the   object that we perceive?*"

This leads us to ignore those causes of the impression that are not candidates for *being* the object perceived—as our perceptual action (in the relevant role) is not. But it may be that something that's not itself a candidate for being the object of perception, can still explain why a certain thing in the chain of causes *is* that object. Such a factor may figure *as a cause of a cause causing* the impression, and point us to the cause it operates upon as the thing perceived. There is no reason to ignore this possibility.

We are apt to look for a distinctive 'way in which' the perceptual object causes the impression, *e.g.* by the reflecting of light from its surface. But again, it may be that what matters, instead, is a distinctive way in which the relevant cause is *caused* to cause that impression, in whatever way it does so. Of course if the penny is caused to cause a tactile impression by our feeling it, then any intermediate cause of that impression, *e.g.* some nervous activity in the fingertips, is also caused by our feeling the penny. But notice that the intermediate cause is *not* caused to cause the impression by our feeling the penny. (What causes the firing of neurons in our fingertips to cause the intermediate neural events in our brains is, for instance, *the intact state of the neural pathways* between the two parts of our body. The perceptual activity of feeling the penny causes the first event—the activity in our fingertips—but it is not what causes that first event to cause the second.)

We do not consider that the answer to Q might cite a cause that is *not itself* the thing that is perceived. We perhaps construe the question Q as if it were this:

> Q1 Which member of the set of causes of the impression causes the impression in such a way that *it* is the object being perceived?

This formulation makes explicit the assumption that the cause with reference to which we identify the object being perceived must be identical with the object being perceived. Again, the assumption is unjustified. A better version of the question will be one free of that assumption, such as this:

> Q2 Which member of the set of causes of the impression causes the impression in such a way that *some* member of that set is thereby identified as (or constituted) the object perceived?

One way in which this distortion of the question happens is that we conceive of a *causal chain* leading to the sensory impression, and the links of this causal chain—as, I think, of any 'causal chain'—are selected by some tacit principle from the plethora of causal factors contributing to the final effect. The causal chain is very much a construction of our own making, and our attention may be trapped arbitrarily inside it. Focused on just the links in the causal chain, we ignore those causes that are not links in it, and that come into the picture as it were from the side. If we are thinking of Price's causal chain, for instance, the act of looking at the table is not a link in the chain, since it is not caused by the prior link of *that* chain, the electric light's shining on the table. (Of course, the act of looking has its own causes and is a link of its own, intersecting, causal chain.)

4 Perception by Direct Contact vs. Indirect Perception

The idea of the object of a perceptual activity and that of the object perceived are correlative ideas. We are exploring the proposition that these objects are identical. (That is, when there *is* a perceptual action involved: there isn't always.) This idea is first suggested by the case of perceptual actions upon objects in which that action is plainly sufficient to identify the object consequently perceived: as the thing we've laid hands on or bitten into. But there is not, in general, any epistemic priority to be assigned to either term of the proposed identity, either to the object of the act or the object perceived. There is no reason why there should be. Sometimes we can discover what we are perceiving *from* our knowledge of our perceptual activities. We may know more about such activities, particularly about our own movements, and what things are affected by them, than we know, independently, about the activities and movements of things whereby they affect our senses. Especially in the case of feeling and tasting, But even here it may be the other way around, that we identify what we are touching, in our pocket, our keys or our lighter, by the feel of it, not by where our fingers are; or what we are tasting in the mouthful of granola, the raisins or the cranberries.

Especially where there is no such 'direct physical contact,' as there is not with hearing and seeing and smelling, there may be no way to identify the object of the perceptual action except by identifying the object perceived. There may be nothing that identifies what you're listening to except the fact that you hear it. This seems a worrying point, though not because it is inconsistent with the identity thesis. It isn't.[17] But it may limit its ability to answer our lead question in as satisfying a way as one might wish.

In these non-contact modalities, the thing perceived acts upon the sentient being from a distance, of course, through the medium of some sensible 'effusion' from the thing—its sound or odor, perhaps the magnetic pull of it, or the light from or reflected by the thing. [18] We noted earlier that the question, 'Which one cause of the percept is the one that is perceived?' is wrongly put, since there are a few such causes, not only one. When one hears the train one also hears the sound of the train. And generally to perceive a thing is also to perceive what earlier I called its presentational quality: to taste a thing is to taste its taste, to feel a thing is to feel its feel. In the case of the non-contact modalities the presentational qualities are the thing's sounding a certain way, its smelling a certain way or its looking a certain way, as it makes or emits or presents the effusing sound, odor, or light.[19] To perceive the thing is to perceive the effusion.

---

[17] There may sometimes be nothing that identifies the morning star except the fact that it's the evening star. (Maybe it's always cloudy in the morning.) Regarding such puzzles about the identity of some x with y, we must keep two questions separate: (1) whether there are distinct 'criteria' for being x and for being y —distinct factors constituting being one or the other—and (2), the question whether there is, in a particular case, evidence available of a thing's being x distinct from that available for its being y.

[18] Hobbes: "... the philosophy schools ... say, for the cause of vision, that the thing seen sendeth forth on every side a visible species, (in English) a visible show, apparition, or aspect, or a being seen." *Leviathan*, Chapter One last paragraph.

[19] If light or its role in seeing is unknown to one who nevertheless knows what seeing is, he might have the cognate concept of a thing's presenting a sight. 'You see the sight of your face

These effusions are of course real physical things, occupying places and travelling through space, information about their source contained in them and flowing with them from place to place. They are things distinct from our sensory consciousness of them, and distinct from the things from which they flow. Nonetheless perceiving such an effusion of a thing is the same as perceiving the thing itself.[20] To smell Dr. Johnson's stench is to smell the man himself, though he has departed and left his stench in the coach, perhaps also his hat. The relevant perceptual *activity* goes on when and where those physical sensibilia may be perceived, and the action is conducted in or on those places. To *know* what stinks (beyond the stench itself) is to discover what's *making* the stench, perhaps by further sniffing, looking, and inference to the best explanation. Similarly for what one is hearing or seeing. Hypotheses about the likely source of the relevant effusion guides subsequent perceptual actions, of the same or of other sense modalities, the results of which confirm or disconfirm those hypotheses. The full story will bring in the whole temporally extended suite of perceptual actions that may be involved, and the temporally extended perception of the objects perceived.

What we may know about the nature of these effusions enters into the matter. The line of sight may sometimes be traced from perceiver straight out to the object being looked at, and thus seen, as was the case with this table. But not always, since light bends and reflects and takes time to travel. To see, indeed to look at, one's own face can only be to look *away* from the location of one's actual face toward the mirror where light reflected from it is reflected back into one's eyes. Seeing a thing is, in a manner of speaking, seeing the light reflected from it, so looking at the mirror one is seeing one's face.[21] Or

---

in the mirror.' 'Sight' is an interesting term, that works in some ways like 'light', in some ways not.

[20] Bishop Berkeley to the contrary notwithstanding: "When I hear a coach drive along the streets, immediately I perceive only the sound ... [though] I am said to hear the coach. Nevertheless, in truth and strictness, nothing can be heard but sound." First Dialogue.

[21] And seeing the mirror as well? We are not seeing the transparent front surface of a glass mirror (if it's clean, and we can't see its shape, etc.). Are we seeing the silvered back surface of that plate of glass? Maybe we aren't seeing that either, though that is what reflects the light we see. For what does it look like? One's face? No. And the silvery look of that surface itself is hidden, if you will, by the colored light it reflects. Hidden by light. Maybe we needn't be seeing the mirror at all, even though we are looking at it. This is no objection (to the main thesis), if this looking does not cause the mirror to cause a visual impression. But it does. It causes an impression, however, of our face, not an impression of the mirror. Must we add a necessary condition, then, for seeing x, that x cause a visual impression of itself. This *of-ness* relation might be defined in terms of the impression's representing properties of x. Such representing is a particular causal relation (in my own view, at least), so the case for a causal analysis of perception would not be compromised. However, such a condition will not do the analytical work the perceptual activity condition might do. For an impression is equally a representation also of those of its nearer causes with which it is isomorphic, e.g. in the retina—again, in my own view

sometimes we see we the light of the thing itself. To see a star is to see its light, wherever in the sky that light may now be, possibly not in the region where the star was, long ago, when it emitted that light.[22] One looks toward the light to see the thing the light is from. To hear a thing is to hear the sound of it, and the act of listening is trained upon the sound. This may mean putting one's ear to the ground. Or, to listen to the sound of a person's voice—perhaps she is off in Timbuktu— may be to press a telephone to your ear, not to cup your ears in the direction of Mali. But then hearing that sound is hearing the person, and the object, or rather the several objects (sound, voice, and person), of the perceptual *action* are the things one hears by listening to that sound.[23]

These considerations all bear on the question whether a perceptual action suffices to identify the object perceived in the case of the non-contact modalities. They involve recognizing the complexity of what is perceived (*e.g.,* a sound *and* the thing making it), and the way we direct the perceptual action upon the distinct elements of what we perceive; how those elements are related one to the other, causally, and even the nature (as commonly conceived) of the element that immediately affects our senses. They appeal also to the complexity of the temporally *extended* perceptual activity (and its object).

But let us return to an isolated perceptual act which causes its object to cause a perception, and ask whether what is perceived, of all the causes involved in causing that percept, can be identified by that act. Are there facts about the internal causal structure of that event and the causal chain in which the action plays its part, that identify the object of that action as what is perceived?

Consider an example offered in discussion by Michael Bratman. You go to the station and listen for the train you are to meet. The train, moving slowly and quietly and still out of earshot, rouses a flock of geese that makes a racket

---

of representation: even if it carries no Dretskean information about such causes. (Compare the case of the mirror to the echoing voice from the canyon *vs.* the bat's information-laden echoes.) For the view of representation mentioned here, see my paper 'Toward a causal theory of linguistic representation', *Midwest Studies in Philosophy*, Vol. II (Minnesota, 1977).

[22] Tim Schroeder brought this up in discussion. (I see that Hobbes uses mirrors and echoes to show that 'colours and sounds' can be separated from 'the objects that cause them.' But he goes on: "Those colours and sounds are in us; for if they were in the bodies or objects that cause them, they couldn't be separated from them.") *Leviathan*, Part 1, Ch. 1, fourth paragraph.

[23] Or so I would say. But there can be an issue about what kinds of transformations an effusion can undergo, while still making genuine hearing or smelling or seeing of its source possible. Fred used to hold that seeing-something-on-television was not seeing it full stop. While this issue was in the air, a Wisconsin state basketball final, broadcast on television, was won by a sixty-foot shot at the buzzer. The next day, over after-seminar martinis, I asked Fred if he had seen that incredible shot. 'Yes!' he said, and I had him. Unmoved, he said I had just tricked him into saying something false.

so loud that this sound *can* be heard. You hear the sound of the geese and therefore the geese, not the train or the sound the train makes. It is the perceptual act of listening (going out on the platform to listen for the train) that causes the sound of the geese to cause your auditory experience. But it also caused the *train* (by rousing the geese) to cause that experience. (The train would not have caused the experience had you stayed in the depot and not gone out to listen for the train.) But you did not hear the train.

So it appears that the following abstract formulation will not do:

(OPOA) the object perceived is a thing C such that the perceptual activity 'done to' or 'directed upon' C caused C to cause the sensory impression to occur.

(The acronym is for Object Perceived is Object of Action.) The problem is that in any causal chain ABCDE, if an event X external to that chain is a cause of C causing E, then *a fortiori* X is also a cause of A causing E.[24] Where the perceptual activity involves no direct contact with one as opposed to others of the causes in the chain—no touching or biting of one of them—then there seems to be nothing to determine *which* cause is the object of the act, nothing to stop the train, as much as the geese, from qualifying as the object of the act of listening: nothing apart from the fact that the train wasn't heard, but we cannot bring that fact into play without circularity.

This is a rather *recherché* sense in which a perceptual activity X causes something to cause an impression. But that gives us no right to ignore it. The intuitive oddness of it may reflect the sense that while X is, in a way, the cause of A causing E, that is only owing to the fact that X causes *C* to cause E. In other words the capacity of X to cause A to cause E depends upon its capacity to cause C to cause E. But not *vice versa*: the capacity of X to cause E does *not* depend upon X's capacity to cause A to cause E. The capacity of your listening to cause the geese to cause your auditory impression did not depend upon the capacity of your listening to cause the train to scare the

---

[24] No similar problem arises for causes further up the chain from the object perceived, e.g. the sound of the geese. Consider causal chain ABCDE. Is it the case, that if an event X external to that chain is a cause of C causing E, then *a fortiori* X is also a cause of D causing E? No. Your listening on the train platform (X) did *not* cause (D) the vibrations of your eardrums to cause (E) the auditory impression. That vibration would have caused the impression no matter what caused the sound that caused the vibration or whether anything at all caused it. Granted, the listening can be said to have caused the vibrations to have caused an impression *of the geese*, for had one *not* been listening and heard the sound of the geese, and something else had caused those same eardrum vibrations and thus the impression, it would not have been an impression *of the geese* that occurred. But this is irrelevant. (OPOA) concerns the causing of the impression's *occurring*, not the cause of the impressions being *of* (representing) the object it is of.

geese—for your listening did *not* cause the train to do anything. Its causal capacity to cause the geese to cause the impression did not depend upon its capacity to cause the train to cause the impression. Distant unperceived causes of the impression might be excluded as candidates for objecthood, then, by a codicil requiring that their causal capacity *not* depend asymmetrically upon the capacity of any nearer item in the causal chain to cause the impression.[25]

Appendix on avoiding circularity

1. The non-cognitivity of simple perception, and of the perceptual activities conceptually involved therein.

I subscribe to the view that there is a fundamental form of perception that is entirely non-cognitive and non-conceptual, expressed by statements of the form 'S perceives 'X' where 'perceives' may be 'sees', 'hears', *etc.*, and 'X' may designate a physical object or event (among other things), and where any expression referring to the object or event may be substituted for 'X' saving truth; and the statement carries no implication that the subject S possesses the concept in terms of which the object is therein described or that S knows what an X is. Let all these logical features be summed up in the adjective "simple."

I've suggested that the objects of simple perception are those causes of the percept that are also objects of relevant perceptual activities on the part of S. The *relevant* perceptual activities I would advert to in attempting to answer the present question are those that are exactly as simple, in the sense indicated, as are the simple perceptual states of seeing or hearing or feeling *etc.* an object. 'S feels (tastes, smells) X' does not change truth-value whatever co-referential expression is substituted for 'X'; and obviously infants and animals without concepts can be S. This is not to deny that (1) these activities may be involved in, and crucial to, the cognitive and concept-applying business of *recognizing* the things we perceive—not just in causing the tactile sensation of the penny but in causing the recognition of it as a penny. Neither is it to deny (2) that there exist descriptions of perceptual activities that may imply certain cognitive or conceptual abilities on the part of the perceiver. 'Listening for' or 'looking for' something plainly do so, unlike 'listening to' or 'looking at', for the former imply some intention to see or hear the designated object, and the usual notional *vs.* directly referential issues arise in the interpretation of the object of 'listening/looking *for*.' We may ignore these issues here. More interestingly, it may be that *some*

---

[25] I see, in looking back into Dretske's *Knowledge and the Flow*, that he had made use of a similar point for a similar purposes. See especially p. 162.

varieties of perceptual activity involve concepts that guide the 'construction' of even the most primitive perceptual representations, perhaps rather as Kant maintained; and that they involve also the use of these concepts, informing 'rules' that govern the sensation-generating activities highlighted in this discussion.[26]

That's another line of work. In the present project, such complex, concept-dependent perceptual activities are not to be brought into the basic analysis; only conception-free activities are to figure in it. This is to avoid circularity. If we were to bring into play perceptual activities that seem logically to require the subject to have a concept of the thing felt or smelt or knowledge of the thing being looked for, then it might be charged that the description of the perceptual activity presupposes the use by the agent of a general concept of *the object* to be perceived by the performance of that act. The concept of such an act might therefore be deemed illegitimate to use in stating an analysis of the concept of the object of perception, for the *analysans* will surreptitiously make use of that very concept. So only 'simple' perceptual activities are to be brought into the analysis.

2. The circularity of an alternative '*quale*-tative' answer.

To answer the title question of this paper one idea that may seem promising involves a necessary condition of simple perception that figured only lightly in the discussion above. It is a necessary condition of perceptually feeling a thing that the thing should *feel* some way or other to the perceiver, and *mutatis mutandis* for the other modes of sensation: the perceived object must look, sound, taste, or smell some way to the perceiver. (A *causal* theory might interpret this condition as meaning that the thing *e.g.* felt must *cause* an impression—sense-datum, percept, *etc.*—in the sensory consciousness of the perceiver, and not just any kind of impression but rather, specifically, one which has the distinctive quality of a *tactile* impression, as opposed to that of a visual impression, *etc.*—thus an impression wherein it *feels e.g.* round as opposed to *looking* round.) So when you actively feel something x, you perceptually feel x, only because it feels, presentationally and *qualia*-wise, some way or other to you. (Suppose your wiring were so fouled up that when you actively felt the penny, it consequently only *looked* a certain way to you: *e.g.*

---

[26] Consider feeling the shape of one tabletop with a circular edge and another with an oval edge. Feeling the two shapes, and the difference between them, would seem to require perceiving kinesthetically the difference between the oval and the circular movement of the fingertip. The kinesthetic impression of moving it in a circular trajectory, as its movement continues to cause the edge of the tabletop to produce a uniform (edgy) tactile sensation, is caused by our moving the hand in such a way, as if in accordance with a rule: continue in a path which continuously yields just such a tactile sensation.

looked round, as a result, rather than *feeling* round. Then you would not be perceptually feeling the penny.)

Now, to answer our question—*which* cause of the impression is the one that one perceives?—might it not do to say the particular cause (of the *e.g.* visual impression) that one sees is the thing that—unlike the *other* causes of the impression—consequently *looks* some way or other to one? The thing one perceptually feels, hears, tastes, or smells is the thing that qualitatively feels, sounds, tastes, or smells a certain way. It is not the neural activity in one's fingertips, or what consequently goes on in one's brain, that feels cool and round and smaller than a nickel and bigger than a dime: of all the links in the causal chain it could only be the penny that feels so.

This line has some appeal. For one thing, it is *necessary* that the thing perceptually felt feels qualitatively some way or other to the perceiver; this is an advantage over the perceptual activity line, because it is *not* necessary that the perceiver actively feels the thing he feels perceptively.

But on closer inspection I think a circle emerges. The problem is that the '*quale*-tative' answer will not do if *which cause it is* that feels a certain way to us is determined by a prior application of the concept of the object of perception. And this seems to be the case. It is clear enough which cause it is that we *conceive* of as feeling a certain way, and which we do not. We conceive of it being the penny, but why do we not conceive of it being a nearer cause, like the neural activity in our fingertips, that feels that way? Of course there is an answer to this: it could not *be* a neural event that is *round*, or *cool*, for instance: there is a category absurdity in such an idea. It could only be such an object as the penny; and therefore only the penny could *feel,* qualitatively, round or cool. But that is because we have *conceived* of the impression, conceived the *quale,* in terms of qualities that might belong only to the kind of thing that we feel (the kind of thing we can *touch*). But if so, then the concept we are seeking to analyze is tacitly being employed in the framing of our conception of the impression and its *qualia*: a prior concept of the thing perceived is being allowed to determine the way we describe the way the impression makes things seem to us. We lack the conceptual vocabulary for this, but, if we consider the tactile impression as it is in itself, it would seem that we might conceive of the impression, and of the way it makes things seem to us, in 'object-neutral' terms— terms that would carry no presuppositions about what it is we are (or might be) feeling, hearing, seeing, *etc.* The point is that the characterization of the way things feel qualitatively to us, serves to single out the item in the causal chain that we perceptually feel only because the conception of the way it feels qualitatively is framed in terms of characteristics that might belong to only a thing of a certain kind or category. We employ a prior notion of what kind of thing the object of perception *is* to conceive those characteristics,[27] which relies upon a prior identification of the particular cause of such an impression that is the object perceived. This fact convicts the '*quale*-tative' answer to our question of circularity.

On the other hand, no such circularity seems to attend the attempt to identify the object perceived as the object of a perceptual action. The categorial *kind* of things that may be felt, or tasted, *i.e.* that may be objects of those physical acts, is determined by the nature just of the *act*.[28] It is not determined by their prior identification as being possible objects of *perceptual* feeling or tasting. The satin can be touched, the peach bitten into, as no neural activity —no event or state—can be, and this is owing to the nature of touching and biting. Similarly, I think, for seeing, hearing, and smelling. The redness and loudness and acridity experienced as sensory *qualia* are properties that can actually characterize such things as we can look at, listen to, and sniff.

Personal note on Fred Dretske

An anecdote from Dennis Stampe:

I worked with and did philosophy with Fred Dretske for twenty five years or so at Wisconsin, starting in 1966. It was suggested that we contributors to this volume write something about our work with Fred—perhaps some important advice we got from him. I couldn't think of any advice, except he did once advise me to do something about my sagging front porch, and I advised him not to buy a house so near the airport. He ignored my advice, and I never fixed the porch. But I did once ask him what he thought of some stuff I was trying to do on properties and predicates. He just shook his head no. I'm sure he was right, even right not to elaborate. Such brusqueness was typical of Fred, at least when he was younger. If he didn't take to an idea (even a good one!) he gave it short shrift. He was not one to offer detailed criticism or commentary on one's work, or advice about how to improve it.

But he had a great influence on us, especially on those of us who were good friends and kept up a bit with one another's work, lunching together practically every day at the Union, dropping in on one another's seminars, often retiring at the end of the day to a dark basement place on State Street called The Grotto, for martinis and more talk. To me, it was the best of philosophical times.

---

[27] Many think that *qualia*, and the properties that characterize them, are in some manner given to us intuitively and inwardly. But that does not mean, and it is implausible to think, that the concepts we employ to characterize those 'entities' (*e.g.* of being bitter or satiny) are similarly given, and in particular given independently of our conception of the properties of the physical bodies (chocolate or satin) that typically cause those entities of consciousness.

[28] Thanks here to Martha Gibson.

Our interaction led to a kinship between my views and Fred's on meaning and content –to 'Wisconsin Semantics' as Jerry Fodor called it. But the kinship was less obvious to us --certainly less obvious to *him*-- than it was to others. I suppose he and I talked about points on which we differed and not the lines of thought we had in common. In any case, none of that work was collaborative in the usual sense, unless there is unconscious collaboration. We certainly never sat down to work on any of it together.

But in retrospect, I can see one link that may be of interest, and illustrates the way Fred's ideas, as they turned over in one's own thinking, might work their influence. This goes back in a general way to his *Seeing and Knowing,* and a seminar of Fred's in 1966 which worked through a draft of the book, but more particularly to an evening seminar in which Fred laid out his conclusive reasons account of knowledge. Peter Unger, in fine form, was on hand for the skeptical opposition. (This must have been in 1969, because after the seminar we went across the street to The Grotto to watch Lew Alcindor in his first year with the Milwaukee Bucks.)

Dretske's account of perceptual knowledge turns on the idea of a set of objective conditions C such that *in* those conditions, it would not look (etc.) to one as if p unless it were the case that p. The belief that p if based on such a perception, occurring in such conditions, could not possibly be false, and therefore one knew that p, even if one did not know that conditions C obtained. This idea, of such objective knowledge-securing conditions, suggests an answer to another question, which I do not think was then on Fred's mind. That is the question What *is* it for a perception E to be such that it looks as if *p*? It suggests this answer: It is for it to be the case that provided that such favorable conditions C should hold, E would not make it look *that* way to the subject if it were not the case that p. Turning this around, and generalizing, to say what E *means* is to identify a certain situation that would obtain, provided those conditions were to obtain; and, if they should *not* obtain, E may *inaccurately* represent the thing one perceives, retaining the non-epistemic, natural relation to that thing that is representation. This question –what determines the 'content' of a perceptual state, its significance or its accuracy conditions?— was, as I say, not a question much on Fred's mind at that point. But meaning had long been my subject and right then, representation and content more generally. I was immersed in the *Tractatus* at just that time and the question what it is for an utterance to say that p, or for an event to show (or seem to show) that p. It occurred to me that *any* representation must afford the provisional or counterfactual possibility of knowing, from it, the thing it represents (the temperature, the age of the tree) —the provision being that there be conditions, 'fidelity' conditions I called them, such that had they obtained the representation, saying or seeming to show that p, would not have been projected had it not been the case that p. (Perhaps in such circumstances nothing else could possibly *cause* it to occur.)

I do not think I then saw that link with Fred's ideas quite clearly. And there were differences: fidelity in my conception might reflect the well-functioning of underlying mechanisms, and this might be crucial to other aspects of meaning. But that apart, my 'fidelity conditions' were pretty much the knowledge-securing conditions of Fred's account. I don't think Fred saw the connection either, or maybe he was just unimpressed by it. For when he directed his attention squarely to the question of content, only some time later, his thinking was dominated by his new concept of information, which reshaped his view of the whole field. The distinctive task of a theory of semantic content, as he saw it, was to account for a signal's containing information in the way the propositional attitudes contain it, so as to attain the highest degree of intentionality. This was not merely would-be information but rather information stripped-down and refined by the distinctive manner of its ('digital') encoding. 'Semantic' meaning was a product of a kind of encoding. In any case, that is the novel idea he'd hit on when he announced to me one day, on our way down to lunch, that he 'now had a theory of content.' Only much later would he condescend to use the idea of the natural *function* of a signal that Berent Enç and I had gone on about for years. But I now think that his earlier approach had more promise, and we ought to have developed it better.

References

Descartes, R. 2017. *Meditations on the First Philosophy.* Cambridge: Cambridge University Press.

Dretske, F. 1969. *Seeing and Knowing.* Chicago: University of Chicago Press.

Dretske, F. 1981. *Knowledge and the Flow of Information.* Cambridge, MA: MIT Press.

Dretske, F. 1969. Perception and Cognition: The Goldilocks Test. *The Cognitive Penetrability of Perception,* eds. J. Zeimbekis and A. Raftopoulos. Oxford: Oxford University Press.

Grice, P. 1965. The Causal Theory of Perception. *Perceiving, Sensing and Knowing,* ed. R. Swartz. New York: Anchor Press.

Hobbes, T. 2009. *Leviathan.* Oxford: Oxford University Press.

Price, H. H. 1932. *Perception.* London: Methuen.

Price, H. H. 1990. The Causal Theory. *Perceiving, Sensing and Knowing,* ed. R. Swartz. New York: Anchor Press.

Warnock, G. 1990. Seeing. *Perceiving, Sensing and Knowing,* ed. R. Swartz. New York: Anchor Press.

Winer, G.A., Cottrell, J.E., Gregg, V.R., Foumier, J.S., & Bica, L.A. 2002. Fundamentally misunderstanding visual perception: Adults' belief in visual emissions. *American Psychologist, 57*:417-424.

Berkeley, G. 1999. Principles of Human Knowledge and Three Dialogues. Oxford: Oxford University Press.

Stampe, D. 1977. Toward a Causal Theory of Linguistic Representation. Midwest Studies in Philosophy, Vol II, ed. P. French, 42-63. Minneapolis: University of Minnesota Press.

Fred Dretske's Publications

Books

Seeing and Knowing, 1969, University of Chicago Press and Routledge and Kegan Paul. Midway Reprint Edition (University of Chicago Press), 1988. Chapter 2, Non-Epistemic Seeing, reprinted in *Philosophie der Wahrnehmung, Modelle und Reflexion*, ed. Lambert Wiesing, Frankfurt; Suhrkamp Verlag, 2002.

Knowledge and the Flow of Information, 1981, A Bradford Book/MIT Press, Cambridge, Mass. (published by Basil Blackwell in England). Chapter 6, Sensation and Perception, reprinted in (a) Dancy, *Perceptual Knowledge*, Oxford University Press, 1988; and (b) *Readings in Epistemology*, ed. Jack S. Crumley II, Mayfield Publishing Co. 1999; Republished in 1999 by CSLI Publications, Stanford University. Chinese Edition: Translation into Chinese and published by The Commercial Press, Beijing, 2013. Spanish Edition: *Conocimiento E Informacion*, 1987, Biblioteca Cientifica Salvat, Barcelona.

Explaining Behavior: Reasons in a World of Causes, 1988, MIT Press, A Bradford Book. Chapter III, Representational Systems, reprinted in *Readings in the Philosophy of Mind*, ed. Tim O'Connor and David Robb, London; Routledge. 2003: 304-330. Japanese edition: Keiso Shobo of Tokyo, published in 2005, translated by Mizumoto Masaharu. Chinese edition: Translated into Chinese and published by The Commercial Press, Ltd, Beijing, 2013.

Naturalizing the Mind, 1995. Cambridge, MA: MIT Press. Chapter 4 translated into German and reprinted in Grundkurs Philosphie Des Geistes. Band 2: Phänomenales Bewusstein, Thomas Metzinger, editor. Mentis, Paderborn (2006), pp. 317-344. German edition: *Naturalisierung des Geistes,* 1998. Schöningh Vrelag of Paderborn. Polish edition: *Naturalizoanie Umyslu,* translated by Barttomiej Swiqtczak, Wydawnictwo Instytutu Filozofii I Socjologii PAN, Warsaw, 2004. Japanese edition: Keiso Shobo of Tokyo, 2007.

Perception, Knowledge, and Belief: Selected Essays. Cambridge University Press, February 2000.

Knowledge: Readings in Contemporary Epistemology. Co-edited with Sven Bernecker. Oxford University Press. 2000.

Articles

[1960-1970]

"Particulars and the Relational Theory of Time," *Philosophical Review,* 70, 4 (October 1961).

"Moving Backward in Time," *Philosophical Review,* 71, 1 (January 1962).

"Observational Terms," Philosophical Review, 73, 1 (January 1964).

"Particular Reidentification," *Philosophy of Science,* 31, 1 (April 1964).

"Reasons and Falsification," *Philosophical Quarterly* (January 1965).

"Counting to Infinity," *Analysis,* Supplementary Volume (January 1965).

"Ziring Ziderata," *Mind* (April 1966).

"Can Events Move?" *Mind* (October 1967).

"Reasons and Consequences," *Analysis* (April 1968).

"Seeing and Justification," and "Reply to Hugly" in *Perception and Personal Identity,* ed. Norman S. Care and Robert H. Grimm, Case Western University Press, 1968.

"Epistemic Operators," *Journal of Philosophy,* 67, 24; pp. 1007-1023 (December 1970); reprinted in *The International Research Library of Philosophy,* ed. John Skorupski, Dartmouth Publishing Co.; reprinted in *Scepticism,* ed. DeRose and Warfield, Oxford Press, 1999.

[1970-1980]

"Conclusive Reasons," *Australasian Journal of Philosophy,* (May 1971). Reprinted in (a) *Essays on Knowledge and Justification,* ed. George Pappas and Marshall Swain, Cornell University Press, Ithaca and London, 1978; (b) translated into German and appearing in *Analytische Philosophie Der Erkenntnis,* ed. Peter Beiri, Athenaum, 1987.

"Reasons, Knowledge and Probability," *Philosophy of Science* (June 1971).

"Perception from an Epistemological Point of View," *Journal of Philosophy* (October 1971).

"Causal Irregularity," (with Aaron Snyder), *Philosophy of Science* (March 1972). Reprinted in *Analytical Metaphysics*, ed. Michael Tooley, Garland Publishing Inc., 1999.

"Contrastive Statements," *Philosophical Review*, 81, 4 (October 1972): 411-437

"Perception and Other Minds," *Nous* (March 1973).

"Causal Sufficiency; A Reply to Beauchamp," (with Aaron Snyder) *Philosophy of Science* (June 1973).

"Explanation in Linguistics," *Explaining Linguistic Phenomena*, ed. David Cohen, Halsted Press, John Wiley and Sons, New York, 1974.

"Perception," *Collier's Encyclopedia*, Macmillan Publishing Company, New York, 1974.

"The Content of Knowledge," *Forms of Representation*, ed. Bruce Freed et al., North Holland; Amsterdam, 1975.

"Referring to Events," *Midwest Studies in Philosophy*, vol. 2, ed. Peter French, Ted Uehling, and Howard Wettstein, University of Minnesota Press; Minneapolis, Minn. 1977.

"Laws of Nature," *Philosophy of Science*, 44, 2 (June 1977); reprinted in (a) *Through Time and Culture: Introductory Readings in Philosophy*, ed. A. Pablo Iannone, Prentice Hall, 1993; (b) *Theory, Evidence and Explanation*, ed. Peer Lipton, (a volume in *The International Research Library of Philosophy*, John Skorupski, general editor) Dartmouth Publishing Co.; Hampshire, England; (c) *Philosophy of Science Readings*, ed. Curd and Cover, University of Chicago Press, 1998; (d) *Analytical Metaphysics*, ed. Michael Tooley, Garland Publishing 1999; (e) *Readings on Laws of Nature*, ed. John Carroll, University of Pittsburgh Press 2004; (f) *Philosophy of Science: An Anthology*, ed. Marc Lange, Blackwell Publishers 2006.

Replies to Mary Hesse ("Truth and the Growth of Scientific Knowledge") and Dudley Shapere ("The Influence of Knowledge on the Description of Facts"), *Proceedings: Philosophy of Science Association*, vol. 2, 1977.

"Causal Theories of Reference," *Journal of Philosophy*, 74, 10 (October 1977).

"Reply to Niiniluoto," *Philosophy of Science*, 45, 3 (September 1978).

"The Role of the Percept in Visual Cognition," *Minnesota Studies in the Philosophy of Science: Perception and Cognition*, vol. 9, ed. Wade Savage, University of Minnesota Press, Minneapolis, Minn. 1978.

"Chisholm on Perceptual Knowledge," *Grazer Philosophische Studien*, vol. 7/8, 1979.

"Simple Seeing," *Body, Mind and Method: Essays in Honor of Virgil Aldrich*, ed. D. F. Gustafson and B. L. Tapscott, D. Reidel, Dordrecht-Holland, 1979. Reprinted in *Mind and Cognition: An Anthology*, ed. William Lycan and Jesse Prinz, Blackwell 2008.

"The Intentionality of Cognitive States," *Midwest Studies in Philosophy*, vol. 5, ed. Peter French, Theodore Uehling, Howard Wettstein, University of Minnesota Press, Minneapolis, Minn. 1980. Reprinted in *The Nature of Mind*, ed. David Rosenthal, Oxford University Press, 1991.

"Meaning and Information," *Concept Formation and Explanation of Behavior*, ed. Robert Hannaford, Ripon College Studies in the Liberal Arts, vol 4, Ripon, Wis. 1980.

[1981-1989]

"The Pragmatic Dimension of Knowledge," *Philosophical Studies*, 40, 3 (November 1981). Reprinted in *Epistemology: Contemporary Readings*, ed. Michael Huemer, Routledge, 2002.

"A Cognitive Cul-de-Sac," *Mind*, 91, 361 (January 1982), pp. 109-111.

"The Informational Character of Representations," commentary on H. L. Roitblat's "The Meaning of Representation in Animal Memory" in *The Behavioral and Brain Sciences*, 5, 3 (September 1982).

"Precis of *Knowledge and the Flow of Information*," for multiple book review in *Behavioral and Brain Sciences*, 6, 1 (March 1983), pp. 55-63. Reprinted in (a) *Naturalized Epistemology*, ed. Hilary Kornblith, A Bradford Book/MIT Press; Cambridge, Mass., 1985; (b) translated into German (by Thomas Metzinger) and published in a textbook on philosophy of mind, 2010.

"Why Information?" response to commentators, *Behavioral and Brain Sciences*, 6, 1 (March 1983), pp. 82-89.

"The Epistemology of Belief," *Synthese*, 55, 1 (April 1983); reprinted in (1) *Doubting: Contemporary Perspectives on Scepticism*, ed. Glenn Ross and Michael Roth, Kluwer Academic Publishing Co., 1990; (2) *Knowledge and Justification*, vol 1, ed. Ernest Sosa, Hampshire, England; Dartmouth Publishing Co.

"Lost Knowledge," (with Palle Yourgrau), *Journal of Philosophy*, 80, 6 (June 1983).

"Constraints and Meaning," commentary on Barwise and Perry, *Situations and Attitudes*, MIT Press (1983) in *Linguistics and Philosophy*, 1985.

"Causal Theories of Knowledge" (with Berent Enc), *Midwest Studies in Philosophy*, ed. French, Uehling and Wettstein, University of Minnesota Press; Minneapolis, Minn. 1984.

Abstract of "Seeing through Pictures," (Reply to Ken Walton) *Nous*, 18, 1 (1984).

"Mentality and Machines," (Presidential Address, APA Western Division), *Proceedings and Addresses of the American Philosophical Association*, 59, 1 (September 1985). Translated into Hebrew and reprinted in (a) *The Philosophical Machine*, ed. Avron Polakow; (b) *Philosophy, Mind and Cognitive Inquiry*, ed. James Fetzer, Kluwer; (c) *Artificial Intelligence and Cognitive Science: Conceptual Issues*, ed. Andy Clark and Josefa Toribio, Garland Publishing Co; Hamden, CT; (d) *Mechanical Bodies, Computational Minds: Artificial Intelligence from Automata to Cyborgs*, ed. Stefano Franchi and Güven Güzeldere, MIT Press (2005).

"Misrepresentation," *Belief*, ed. Radu Bogdan, Oxford University Press; Oxford, England, 1986. Reprinted in (a) *Mind and Cognition: A Reader*, ed. William Lycan, Oxford; Basil Blackwell; (b) *Readings in Philosophy and Cognitive Science*, ed. Alvin Goldman, MIT Press, 1993; (c) *Mental Representations: A Reader*, ed. Stephen Stich and Ted Warfield, Blackwell, Oxford, 1993; (d) *Philosophie l'esprit: une anthologie*, ed. Denis Fisette and Pierre Poirier, Presses de l'Universite Laval and Librairie Philosophique J. Vrin.; (e) translated into Polish and appearing in a special issue of *Przeglad Filozoficzno-Literacki*, ed. Marcin Milkowski, 2013.

"Aspects of Cognitive Representation," *Problems in the Representation of Knowledge and Belief*, ed. Myles Brand and Mike Harnish, University of Arizona Press; Tucson, Arizona, 1986.

"Minds, Machines and Meaning," *Philosophy and Technology II: Information Technology and Computers in Theory and Practice*, ed. Carl Mitchum, D. Reidel, 1986.

"Stalking Intentionality," (comments on Ken Sayre) *The Behavioral and Brain Sciences*, 9, 1 (March 1986).

"The Explanatory Role of Content," in *Contents of Thought: Proceedings of the 1985 Oberlin Colloquium in Philosophy*. Tucson, Arizona; Univesity of Arizona Press, 1988.

"Bogdan on Information," in *Mind and Language*, 3, 2 (Summer, 1988).

"The Stance Stance," *Behavioral and Brain Sciences*, 11, 3 (September 1988) (Comments on Dennett).

"Reasons and Causes," *Philosophical Perspectives*, vol 3, *Philosophy of Mind and Action Theory*, ed. James Tomberlin; Atascadero, Ca., Ridgeview Publishing Company, 1989.

"The Need to Know," in *Theory of Knowledge: The State of the Art*, ed. Keith Lehrer and Marjorie Clay, University of Arizona Press, 1989.

"Seeing, Believing and Knowing," Chapter 5 in *An Invitation to Cognitive Science*, vol. 2, *Visual Cognition and Action*, ed. Dan Osherson, Stephen Kosslyn and John Hollerbach, Cambridge, Mass.; MIT Press, 1990.

"Putting Information to Work," *Information, Language, and Cognition: Vancouver Studies in Cognitive Science*, ed. Philip Hanson, Vancouver, B.C.; University of British Columbia Press, 1990. Reprinted in *Language and Meaning in Cognitive Science: Cognitive Issues and Semantic Theory*, ed. Josefa Toribio and Andy Clark, New York, Garland Publishing Company 1998.

"Does Meaning Matter?" in *Information, Semantics and Epistemology*, ed. Enrique Villanueva, Blackwell, 1990. Reprinted in *The Philosophy of Psychology: Debates on Psychological Explanation*, ed. Cynthia and Graham Macdonald, Oxford: Blackwell, 1995.

[1990-1999]

"Precis" (of *Explaining Behavior*) and "Reply to Reviewers" (Stich, Millikan, Tuomela, Stampe, Bratman), *Philosophy and Phenomenological Research*, 50, 4 (June 1990).

"Dretske's Replies" in *Dretske and his Critics*, ed. Brian McLaughlin, 180-221. Oxford: Basil Blackwell, 1991.

"How Beliefs Explain Behavior: Reply to Baker," *Philosophical Studies*, 63 (1991), pp.113-117.

"Conscious Acts and Their Objects," (commentary on Velmans' "Is Human Information Processing Conscious?" *Behavioral and Brain Sciences*, vol. 14, no. 4, (December 1991).

"Two Conceptions of Knowledge: Rational vs. Reliable Belief," *Grazer Philosophische Studien*, vol. 40 (1991), pp.15-30.

"The Fragility of Reason" (a critical study of Steve Stich's *The Fragmentation of Reason*), *Dialogue* 31 (1992), pp. 311-20.

"What Isn't Wrong with Folk Psychology," *Metaphilosophy*, vol. 23, no. 1 and 2 (January/April 1992), pp. 1-13.

"The Metaphysics of Freedom," *Canadian Journal of Philosophy*, vol. 22, no. 1 (March 1992), pp. 1-14.

"Mental Events as Structuring Causes of Behavior," in ed. Mele and Heil, *Mental Causation*, Oxford University Press, 1993, pp. 121-136.

"The Nature of Thought," *Philosophical Studies*, 68, pp. 81-95, 1993. Reprinted in *Sprache und Denken*, Walter de Gruyter Verlag; Berlin/New York, ed. Edi Marbach and Alex Burri, 1997.

"Conscious Experience", *Mind*, vol. 102, 406 (April 1993), pp. 1-21. Reprinted in (a) *Consciousness*, MIT press, ed. Block, Flanagan, and Guzeldere; (b) *Consciousness*, ed. Frank Jackson, a volume in the *International Research Library of Philosophy*, Ashgate Publishing Co; Hampshire, England; (c) *Vision and Mind: Selected Readings in the Philosophy of Perception*, ed. Alva Noe and Evan Thompson, MIT Press, 2002; (d) *Philosophy of Mind: Classical and Contemporary Readings*, ed. David Chalmers, Oxford University Press, 2002; (3) Translated into Portuguese by Cicero Barrosa and published in his anthology on consciousness in Brazil 2012.

"Can Intelligence be Artificial?" *Philosophical Studies*, 71 (1993), pp. 201-216.

"Perceptual Knowledge" and "Sensation/Cognition Distinction" for *Companion to Epistemology*, ed. Jonathan Dancy and Ernest Sosa, Blackwell, 1994.

"Mind and Brain," in *The Mind-Body Problem: A Guide to the Current Debate*, ed. Richard Warner and Tadeusz Szubka, Basil Blackwell, 1994.

"Self Portrait," in *A Companion to the Philosophy of Mind*, ed. Samuel Guttenplan, 259-265. Oxford: Basil Blackwell, 1994.

"Modes of Perceptual Representation," *Philosophy and the Cognitive Sciences: Proceedings of the 16th International Wittgenstein Symposium*, ed. Barry Smith, Roberto Casati, and Graham White. Vienna: Holder-Pichler-Tempsky, 1994.

"Introspection," *Aristotelian Society Proceedings*, Spring 1994.

"Reply to Slater and Garcia-Carpintero," *Mind and Language*, 9, 2 (June 1994).

"If You Can't Make One, You Don't Know How it Works," *Midwest Studies in Philosophy*, vol. 19, ed. Peter French, Theodore Uehling, and Howard Wettstein, Notre Dame, IN; University of Notre Dame Press, 1994, pp. 468-482. Reprinted as "A Recipe for Thought" in *Philosophy of Mind: Classical and Contemporary Readings*, ed. David Chalmers, Oxford University Press (2002).

"The Explanatory Role of Information," *Philosophical Transactions. Royal Society, London*, 1994, pp. 1-13.

"Differences that Make No Difference," *Philosophical Topics*, vol. 22, no. 1 and 2 (1994), pp. 41-57.

"Perception" and "Sensibilia" for *Dictionary of Philosophy*, Cambridge: Cambridge University Press, ed. Robert Audi, 1995.

"Causal Relevance and Explanatory Exclusion: Reply to Kim," in *The Philosophy of Psychology: Debates on Psychological Explanation*, ed. Cynthia and Graham Macdonald, Oxford: Blackwell, 1995.

Eleven entries (perception, sensation, percept, awareness, etc.) for *Oxford Companion to Philosophy*, ed. Ted Honderich, 1995.

"Meaningful Perception," revision of "Seeing, Knowing and Believing" for 2nd Edition of *Invitation to Cognitive Science*, vol. 2, Visual Cognition, ed. Stephen Kosslyn, 1995.

"Dretske's Awful Answer," reply to Robert Almeder's "Dretske's Dreadful Question," in *Philosophia*, vol. 24, no. 3-4 (December 1995), pp. 459-464.

"Phenomenal Externalism: If Meanings ain't in the Head, Where are Qualia?" *Philosophical Issues*, 7 (1996), ed. Enrique Villanueva, Ridgeview Publishing Company; Atascadero, CA. pp. 143-158.

"Action and Autonomy," *The Cosmos of Science*, ed. John Earman and John D. Norton, University of Pittsburgh Press, 1996.

"Reply to Melnlyk and Noordhof," *Mind and Language*, vol. 11, 2 (June 1996), 223-228.

"Absent Qualia," *Mind and Language*, vol. 11, no. 1, 1996, pp. 78-85.

"What Good is Consciousness?" *Canadian Journal of Philosophy*, 27, 1 (March 1997), 1-14. Reprinted in *Bewusstsein und Repraesentation*, ed. Frank Esken and Heinz-Dieter Heckmann, Verlag Ferdinand Schoeningh, Paderborn Germany, 1997.

"The Mind's Awareness of Itself," *Bewusstsein und Repraesentation*, ed. Frank Esken and Heinz-Dieter Heckmann, Verlag Ferdinand Schoeningh, Paderborn Germany, 1997; also in *Philosophical Studies*, 95, pp. 103-124, 1999, Peter McInerney, guest editor.

"Minds, Machines, and Money: What Really Explains Behavior." in *Human Action, Deliberation and Causation*, Philosophical Studies Series 77. ed. Jan Bransen and Stefaan Cuypers, Dordrecht: Kluwer Academic Publishers (1998), pp. 157-173.

"Information Theory and Epistemology," for *Routledge Encyclopedia of Philosophy*, ed. Taylor and Francis, 1998.

"Informational Semantics," *MIT Encyclopedia of the Cognitive Sciences* (MITECS), 1998.

"Where is the Mind When the Body Performs?" part of a symposium on *The Athlete's Body*, Stanford University, published in *Stanford Humanities Review*, 6, 2 (1998), pp. 84-88.

"Machines, Plants, and Animals: The Origins of Agency," *Erkenntnis*, 51, pp. 19-31, 1999. Reprinted (translated into German) in *Handlungen und Handlugsgruende (Actions and Reasons for Action)*, ed. Ralf Stoecker, Mentis Verlag GmbH., 2002.

"Mental Causation," *Metaphysics*, vol. 2, *The Paideia Project: Proceedings of the 20th World Congress of Philosophy*, 1999.

[2000-2009]

"Reply to Lopes," *Philosophy and Phenomenological Research*, 60, no. 2 (March 2000), pp. 455-460.

"Entitlement: Epistemic Rights without Epistemic Duties," *Philosophy and Phenomenological Research*, 60, 3 (May 2000), pp. 591-606; published in German, "Berechtigung: Epistemische Rechte Ohne Epistemische Pflichten?" in *Erkenntnestheorie: Positionen Zwischen Tradition and Gegenwart*, ed. Thomas Grundmann, Paderhorn; Mentis. pp. 53-71.

"Where is the Mind?" in *Explaining Beliefs: Lynne Rudder Baker and her Critics* by ed. Anthonie Meijers. Stanford: CSLI Publications 2001, 39-50.

"Norms, History, and the Mental" in *Naturalism, Evolution and Mind*, ed. by Denis Walsh, Cambridge University Press 2001. Reprinted in *Perception, Knowledge, and Belief: Selected Essays*, Cambridge University Press, February 2000.

"Burge on Mentalistic Explanations: or Why I am Still Epiphobic" pp. 115-123 in *Reflections and Replies: Essays on the Philosophy of Tyler Burge*, ed. Martin Hahn and Bjorn Ramberg. MIT Press, 2003.

"Knowing What You Think vs. Knowing That You Think" in *The Externalist Challenge: New Studies on Cognition and Intentionality*, Walter de Gruyter, Berlin, ed. Richard Schantz, 2003 [also published in *Persons, an Interdisciplinary Approach*, Proceedings of the Wittgenstein Conference, 2002, vol. 31, ed. C. Kanzian, J. Quitteter, and E. Runggaldier.]

"The Intentionality of Perception," in *John Searle: Contemporary Philosophy in Focus*. ed. Barry Smith, Cambridge University press, 2003: pp. 154-168.

"Externalism and Self Knowledge," in *Semantic Externalism, Skepticism and Self-Knowledge*, ed. Susana Nuccetelli, MIT Press, 2003.

"Skepticism: What Perception Teaches" in *The Skeptics: Contemporary Essays*, ed. Steven Luper, Ashgate Publishing Co., 2003.

"How Do You Know You Are Not A Zombie?" *Privileged Access and First-Person Authority*, ed. Brie Gertler, Ashgate Publishing Co, 2003. Also published in Portuguese, Conference on Mind and Action III, ed. João Sàáguand, Lisbon, Portugal, 2001.

"Experience as Representation," in *Philosophical Issues*, vol. 13, 2003, *Nous: Annual Supplement, Philosophy of Mind*, ed. Ernest Sosa and Enrique Villanueva. Oxford: Blackwell: 67-82.

"Psychological vs. Biological Explanations of Behavior," *Behavior and Philosophy*, 31 (2003), pp. 1-11. Reprinted in *Philosophy of Action: An Anthology*, eds. Jonathan Dancy and Constantine Sandis, Blackwell, (2015).

"Change Blindness," *Philosophical Studies*, 120: 1-18 (2004).

"Externalism and Modest Contextualism," *Erkenntnis* 61: 173-186, 2004.

"Mental Causation," *Think*, 7 (2004): 6-15.

The Case Against Closure" (pp. 13-26) and "Reaction" (pp. 43-46) (to John Hawthorne), *Contemporary Debates in Epistemology*, ed. Ernest Sosa and Matthias Steup, Blackwell 2005.

"Minimal Rationality," in *Rational Animals?*, ed. Susan Hurley and Mathew Nudds, Oxford University Press, 2006. Translated and reprinted into German in *Der Geist der Tiere*, ed. D. Perler and M. Wild, Suhrkamp Publishers, 2005.

"Perception without Awareness," in *Perceptual Experience*, ed. Tamar Gendler and John Hawthorne, Oxford University Press, 2006. Reprinted in *Mind and Cognition: An Anthology*, ed. William Lycan and Jesse Prinz, Blackwell 2008.

"The Epistemology of Pain," *Pain: New Essays on Its Nature and the Methodology of its Study*, ed. Murat Aydede, MIT Press, 2006.

"Epistemology and Information," in *Philosophy of Information: A Handbook of the Philosophy of Science*, ed. Pieter Adriaans and Johan van Benthem, Elsevier Publishers, 2006.

"Information and Closure," *Erkenntnis* 2006, vol. 64, 409-414.

"Representation, Teleosemantics, and the Problem of Self-Knowledge," in *Teleosemantics?*, ed. Macdonald and Papineau, Oxford University Press, 2006, pp. 69-84.

"What Change Blindness Teaches About Consciousness," *Philosophical Perspectives: Philosophy of Mind*, John Hawthorne, ed. Blackwell, 2007.

"The Metaphysics of Information," Invited address at 30th Wittgenstein Conference, 2007, published in ed. A. Pichler & H. Hrachovec, *Wittgenstein and the Philosophy of the Information: Vol. 1*. Proceedings of the 30th International Ludwig Wittgenstein-Symposium in Kirchberg am Wechsel, Austria 2007. Publications of the Austrian Ludwig Wittgenstein Society *New Series*, vol. 7. (D) Frankfurt a.M.: Ontos.

"What Must Actions be for Reasons to Explain Them?" in *New Essays on the Explanation of Action*, ed. Constantine Sandis, Palgrave 2008.

"Information, Computation, and Cognition," *The Philosophy of Computing and Information: 5 Questions*, ed. Luciano Floridi. Automatic Press/VIP, London and New York, 2008. Translated into Spanish by Julio Ostale and published in *Agora: Papeles De Filosofia*.

Essay in *Epistemology: 5 Questions*, 2008, ed. Vincent Hendricks and Duncan Pritchard, Automatic Press/VIP, London and New York.

"Information-Theoretic Semantics," *The Oxford Handbook of Philosophy of Mind*, ed. Brian McLaughlin, Ansgar Beckermann, and Sven Walter, Oxford University Press, 2009.

Essay in *Mind and Consciousness: 5 Questions*, ed. Patrick Grim, Automatic Press/VIP, London and New York. 2009.

[2010-2015]

"Knowing It Hurts," in *Topics in Contemporary Philosophy*, vol. 5, ed. Michael O'Rourke, MIT Press, 2010.

"Self Profile" for *Companion to Epistemology*, 2nd Edition (2010), ed. Matthias Steup, Jonathan Dancy, Ernest Sosa, and Matthias Steup, Wiley & Blackwell.

"What We See: The Texture of Conscious Experience," in *Perceiving the World*, Bence Nanay, ed. New York: Oxford University Press, 2010.

"Triggering and Structuring Causes," *Blackwell Companion to the Philosophy of Action*, ed. Constantine Sandis and Timothy O'Conner, Blackwell, 2010.

"Chris Hill's *Consciousness*" (book symposium with Ned Block, Alex Byrne and Chris Hill at APA, Pacific Division, April 2011), *Philosophical Studies*.

"I Think I Think, Therefore I Am—I Think" in Liu and J. Perry, *Consciousness and the Self: New Essays*, Cambridge University Press, 2012.

"Doubts About *Cogito*" in *Facets of Self-Consciousness*, ed. Katja Crone, Kritina Musholt, and Anna Strasser, pp. 1-17 of *Grazer Philophische Studien*, 84, (2012).

"Awareness and Authority: Skeptical Doubts about Self-Knowledge," *Introspection and Consciousness*, ed. Declan Smithies and Daniel Stoljar, Oxford University Press, 2012.

"Challenging Closure: Is it a Way to Answer the Skeptic?" *The Harvard Review of Philosophy*, 2012, 19:61-68.

"Skeptical Doubts About Self-Knowledge," in *Routledge Companion to Epistemology*, ed. Sven Bernecker and Duncan Pritchard, 2013.

"Justified True Belief," *The Philosopher's Magazine*, 2013, 61:31-36.

"Perception vs. Conception: The Goldilocks Test," *The Cognitive Penetrability of Perception: New Philosophical Perspectives*, ed. J. Zeimbekis and Athanassios Raftopoulos, Oxford: Oxford University Press, 2015.

"Supervenience and the Causal Explanation of Behavior" in "*Qualia and Mental Causation in a Physical World: Themes from the Philosophy of Jaegwon Kim,*" ed. Terry Horgan, Maracelo Sabatés, and David Sosa, Cambridge University Press, 2015.

Index